PRAYERS OF DAVID

Rabbi Dr. Sidney Vineburg

Library of Congress Control Number: 2017946591

Produced with the assistance of Hudson Bible (www.HudsonBible.com).

ISBN: 978-1-94547-015-8

Cover design by Gearbox | studiogearbox.com

Cover image by Renata Sedmakova | Shutterstock.com

Printed in the United States of America

17 18 19 20 21 22 LBM 1 2 3 4 5 6 7 8

Dedication

For my wife, Devorah Hannah,
our children, and our grandchildren.

"For the sake of my family and friends,
I will say,
'Peace be within you.'"
                    (Psalm 122:8, NIV)

Introduction

A mong the great heroes of the Bible, few stand taller than David. His story reads like a real-life rags-
to-riches tale: Poor shepherd boy from an obscure town
makes good. As a teen, he kills a giant and becomes a war
hero. After years on the run, he serves as the greatest king
in Israel. Throw in David's skills as a master musician and
poet, and you've got a picture of a genuine renaissance man.

But for all his great accomplishments, David struggles. The man who slays physical giants wrestles with
emotional giants that often overwhelm him. At various
times in his life, he lacks integrity, displays arrogance,
alienates his family, and surrenders to the darker corners
of his character.

In response to these moments, David typically turns
to prayer. And those heartfelt expressions are probably

what continue to make his story so appealing to modern readers. We recognize his mistakes, relate to his failures, and share his pain.

David's magnificent prayers found in the Bible serve as excellent examples of the beauty that characterizes ancient Hebrew literature. *Prayers of David* examines forty of his prayers that touch on a variety of topics, such as seeking personal guidance, dealing with injustice, celebrating victories, and finding forgiveness. Each reading also concludes with a traditional Jewish prayer.

This book will help you understand David and his struggles better. But it will also help you see that the more things change, the more they truly stay the same. Readers today can still enjoy the eloquence of David's words—and probably relate to the things that drove him to his knees.

Humility and Leadership

And it came to pass after this, that David inquired of the LORD, saying: "Shall I go up into any of the cities of Judah?" And the LORD said unto him: "Go up." And David said: "Whither shall I go up?" And He said: "Unto Hebron." So David went up thither, and his two wives also, Ahinoam the Jezreelitess, and Abigail the wife of Nabal the Carmelite. And his men that were with him did David bring up, every man with his household; and they dwelt in the cities of Hebron. And the men of Judah came, and they there anointed David king over the house of Judah.

And they told David, saying: "The men of Jabesh-gilead were they that buried Saul." And David sent messengers unto the men of Jabesh-gilead, and said unto them: "Blessed be ye of the LORD, that ye have shown this kindness unto your lord, even unto Saul, and have buried him. And now the LORD show kindness and truth unto you; and I also will requite you this kindness, because ye have done this thing. Now therefore let your hands be strong, and be ye valiant; for Saul your lord is dead, and also the house of Judah have anointed me king over them." (2 Samuel 2:1–7)

I n his classic book on businesses, *Good to Great*, author Jim Collins lists humility as a character trait that makes great leaders. The reason, he suggests, is because humble "leaders channel their ego needs away from themselves and into the larger goal of building a great company."[1]

David is often considered a great leader in Jewish tradition, in part because he displayed courage even at an early age. Possibly the most famous example of this is the story of his victory over Goliath, in 1 Samuel 17.

But an often-overlooked leadership trait in David is his tendency to exhibit genuine humility before God. Even after serious mistakes, such as his adultery with Bathsheba (2 Samuel 11), David humbles himself before God and confesses (2 Samuel 12:13; Psalm 51). And as a leader, David often portrays humility in his vulnerable, heartfelt prayers for God's guidance.

This is evident in the words of David's prayer in 2 Samuel 2:1, which highlight David's trusting posture and humble attitude before God: "Shall I go up into any

---

1   Jim Collins, *Good to Great* (New York: HarperCollins, 2001), 21.

of the cities of Judah?" and "Wither shall I go up?" In seeking God's counsel, perhaps he recognizes his insufficiency. Longing to do what is right for his people, as opposed to pursuing his ego, he stops and looks to God for help. He is neutral regarding God's direction one way or another.

Understanding the context of this prayer is helpful. King Saul and three of his sons—including Jonathan—are dead (1 Samuel 31:1–2). The Israelites are divided between Judah and Israel. At the time of this prayer, David is on the threshold of being named king over Judah, but one of Saul's sons, Ish-bosheth, is made king of Israel (2 Samuel 2:8–9).

David is faced with significant decisions. Rather than turn to his advisors or blindly trust in his own perspective, David in humility asks God if he should go to the towns of Judah to take up the throne. Then God instructs him to go to Hebron, and David humbly follows God's leading. And it is at Hebron that David is acclaimed king over Judah (2 Samuel 2:4).

As we reflect on King David's prayer for guidance, we can see that David's attributes of a leader are found not just in his courageous moments but also in those occasions when he humbles himself and relies on God's guidance and mercy. By contrast, his leadership proves disastrous in those times when he acts in pride. This occurred when, against God's will, he took a census of the people and his military (1 Chronicles 21).

According to Jewish legend, David listened to his advisors and human counselors by day and studied the Torah (the five books of Moses) most of the night, as he sought guidance from God.

Just as David prayed for guidance at a watershed moment in his life, we can contemplate our own approach to making decisions about work and family. This prayer of David can be seen as a reminder to pause and humble our hearts before we rush into choices.

PRAYER

Avinu shebashamayim, our Father in heaven, you guided David to be a great leader and king. Help me to reach out to you for guidance in good times and bad. Help ground my work and life in your teaching. Guide me back to you in repentance and love when I stray. Grant me your foresight and wisdom to be a leader in my home, my community, and my country. May we seek wisdom. As David's son Solomon prayed, "Give me wisdom and knowledge, that I may lead this people" (2 Chronicles 1:10, NIV). Amen.

PRAYERS OF DAVID

Prayer for the Fulfillment of God's Promise
and Covenant: **2 Samuel 7:18–29**

Be Thankful and Share

Then David the king went in, and sat before the LORD; and he said: "Who am I, O Lord GOD, and what is my house, that Thou hast brought me thus far? And this was yet a small thing in Thine eyes, O Lord GOD; but Thou hast spoken also of Thy servant's house for a great while to come; and this too after the manner of great men, O Lord GOD. And what can David say more unto Thee? for Thou knowest Thy servant, O Lord GOD. For Thy word's sake, and according to Thine own heart, hast Thou wrought all this greatness, to make Thy servant know it. Therefore Thou art great, O LORD God; for there is none like Thee, neither is there any God beside Thee, according to all that we have heard with our ears. And who is like Thy people, like Israel, a nation one in the earth, whom God went to redeem unto Himself for a people, and to make Him a name, and to do for Thy land great things and tremendous, even for you, [in driving out] from before Thy people, whom Thou didst redeem to Thee out of Egypt, the nations and their gods? And Thou didst establish to Thyself Thy people Israel to be a people unto Thee for ever; and Thou, LORD, becamest their God. And now, O LORD God, the word that Thou hast spoken concerning Thy servant, and concerning his house, confirm Thou it for ever, and do as Thou hast spoken. And let Thy name be magnified for ever, that it may be said: The LORD of hosts is God over Israel; and the house of Thy servant David shall be established before Thee. For Thou, O LORD of hosts, the God of Israel, hast revealed to Thy servant, saying: I will build thee a house; therefore hath Thy servant taken heart to pray this prayer unto Thee. And now, O Lord GOD, Thou alone art God, and Thy words are truth, and Thou hast promised this good thing unto Thy servant; now therefore let it please Thee to bless the house of Thy servant, that it may continue for ever before Thee; for Thou, O Lord GOD, hast spoken it; and through Thy blessing let the house of Thy servant be blessed for ever." (2 Samuel 7:18–29)

Social researchers and psychologists are finding that the practice of thankfulness can lead to joy and emotional health. Giving thanks helps to move people from bitterness and depression to joy and optimism.

In this prayer, David is expressing his overwhelming gratitude for all that God has done for him. By looking closely at the prayer, we can gain a richer understanding of the importance of thankfulness in our own lives.

David utters this prayer during a time of peace for the Israelites (2 Samuel 7:1). David dwells in a palace made of cedar (2 Samuel 7:2). He is very concerned that while he has a fine house, the ark of the covenant (the ancient dwelling place of God) continues to be housed in a tent, as it had been since the time of Moses (Exodus 31:1–11).

So David consults with his court prophet and advisor, Nathan, and proposes a plan to build a great temple for the ark, a permanent dwelling for God that is even larger and more glorious than David's palace. Nathan initially approves David's plan (2 Samuel 7:2–3). However, during the night, God speaks to Nathan, reminding him that God does not need shelter or a house.

Because of David's thoughtfulness, God blesses David and gives him a covenant that extends to his heirs. In this covenant, God promises to plant the people of Israel eternally in their land (2 Samuel 7:10) and to build for David a "house" (*bayit*, "dynasty") that will rule over Israel forever: "And your house and your kingdom shall be established forever before you. Your throne shall be established forever" (2 Samuel 7:16, NKJV). God also promises that a temple to God will be built—not by David, however, but by his successor, King Solomon (2 Samuel 7:12–14).

In his response to the generous covenant and promise of God, David acknowledges that he has done nothing to merit the great things God has already done for him (2 Samuel 7:18–19). David struggles to express his gratitude (verse 20). He can't believe God would do this for him. In his awe, he praises the God of salvation, who brought the Israelites out of bondage and settled them in the land of Israel (verses 22–24). Finally, in abject humility, David finds the courage to ask for *brachot* (blessings) on himself and his house (verses 27–29).

Although David hoped to build a temple for God, God instead grants David his own house, a dynasty. David offered to build a physical house for God, but in return, God gives him a "house" that is spiritual and generational. This "house" will last even longer than Solomon's Temple.

It is not hard for us to understand David's reaction. Any of us, given an unmerited gift of great value, would likely feel the awe and speechlessness that David experiences. Moreover, David expresses his gratitude by seeking to see God's name and reputation become more widely known in the world. In his prayer he says, "Thy name be magnified for ever" (verse 26). This indicates that David is seeking to use God's gift for purposes greater than just himself.

As we reflect on this prayer, we can pause and consider all the good things we have received and respond with gratitude and humility. In addition, David's prayer can inspire us to share what we've received as a gift with others. As David reminds us in Psalm 41:1, "Blessed is the one who considers the poor!" (ESV).

Eloheinu v'Elohei Avoteinu, our God and God of our ancestors, you are the faithful king of the world. We ask for our families and ourselves the covenant you promised King David, a promise of peace, wholeness, faithfulness and your love. As David prayed, "Your covenant is trustworthy, and you have promised these good things to your servant. Now be pleased to bless the house of your servant, that it may continue forever in your sight; for you, Sovereign LORD, have spoken, and with your blessing the house of your servant will be blessed forever" (2 Samuel 7:28–29, NIV). Amen.

Leaving a Legacy

Wherefore David blessed the LORD before all the congregation; and David said: "Blessed be Thou, O LORD, the God of Israel our father, for ever and ever. Thine, O LORD, is the greatness, and the power, and the glory, and the victory, and the majesty; for all that is in the heaven and in the earth is Thine; Thine is the kingdom, O LORD, and Thou art exalted as head above all. Both riches and honour come of Thee, and Thou rulest over all; and in Thy hand is power and might; and in Thy hand it is to make great, and to give strength unto all. Now therefore, our God, we thank Thee, and praise Thy glorious name. But who am I, and what is my people, that we should be able to offer so willingly after this sort? for all things come of Thee, and of Thine own have we given Thee. For we are strangers before Thee, and sojourners, as all our fathers were: our days on the earth are as a shadow, and there is no abiding. O LORD our God, all this store that we have prepared to build Thee a house for Thy holy name cometh of Thy hand, and is all Thine own. I know also, my God, that Thou triest the heart, and hast pleasure in uprightness. As for me, in the uprightness of my heart I have willingly offered all these things; and now have I seen with joy Thy people, that are present here, offer willingly unto Thee. O LORD, the God of Abraham, of Isaac, and of Israel, our fathers, keep this for ever, even the imagination of the thoughts of the heart of Thy people, and direct their heart unto Thee; and give unto Solomon my son a whole heart, to keep Thy commandments, Thy testimonies, and Thy statutes, and to do all these things, and to build the palace, for which I have made, provision." (1 Chronicles 29:10–19)

M any people hope to leave something good behind for the next generation—to leave a legacy.

This human desire can be seen in this prayer by King David. By looking closely at David's prayer, as he contemplates the succession of his son Solomon, we can enrich our understanding of what it means to leave a legacy.

The context of this prayer is connected to David's desire to build a temple for God, a dream that God doesn't allow David to fulfill. Instead, God gives that task to Solomon (1 Chronicles 22:6–10). In response, as shown so beautifully in this prayer, David decides to release control of his aspirations to God and his son.

Before offering this prayer, David gathers all the officials of Israel, including military commanders and palace officials. Then he addresses Solomon, imploring him, "Solomon my son, know the God of your father and serve him with a whole heart and with a willing mind" (1 Chronicles 28:9, ESV). David expresses his longing for his son to carry on the faith and serve the people of Israel with integrity.

However, these longings are tempered by some harsh realities. David's family life was rarely easy. He had several children by different wives, and they did not always follow God. His son Absalom led a military rebellion against David. At the time of this prayer, David's son Adonijah had declared himself king over Solomon and gathered a following.

Moreover, David recognizes that Solomon is "young and inexperienced" (1 Chronicles 29:1, ESV). Did David worry that his inexperienced son would not be ready for the task? If so, how did he handle that? We can't know everything that transpired in David's heart and mind, but his prayer shows him focusing on four things.

First, David recognizes that God is "exalted as head above all" (verse 11). This implies that David knows his future legacy is ultimately in God's hands. Despite his concerns and fears, David doesn't seem to focus on the problems and dangers that are out of his control. Instead, he turns his eyes to God, recognizes God's authority, and prays.

David also responds in humility, asking, "But who am I, and what is my people?" (verse 14). He recognizes life's brevity, saying, "For we are strangers [*gerim*] . . . and sojourners [*toshavim*], as all our fathers were: our days on the earth are like a shadow, and there is no abiding" (verse 15). In the face of his finite existence, and in recognition of his limitations, he entrusts the temple project to

God. In this prayer, we find an opportunity to ask how we might best respond to our own limitations.

Then David prays that God would protect and support his son Solomon, who will carry David's legacy forward. David seems to recognize that Solomon's character will be paramount in his ability to lead the nation. He asks God to give Solomon "a whole heart" to keep God's commandments (verse 19). In terms of our legacies, the prayer brings attention to the importance of trustworthiness among those who assume responsibility for what we've established and planned.

Finally, David offers his wealth to help build the temple, a project that he would never see completed (verses 2–5, 17). It was an act of faith. David's generosity inspired others to give to the project (verses 6–9). Even at the end of his life, David makes a lasting contribution by giving his wealth for God's purposes.

PRAYER

Eloheinu v'Elohei Avoteinu, our God and God of our ancestors, grant us the blessings you gave to David. Make us worthy of your guidance. Help us to raise our children to know and love you. Grant that we may be examples of compassion, love, tolerance, and generosity so that we are worthy of our children and raise worthy children. May they, like King Solomon, be faithful so that they may build your community of shalom, of peace. Amen.

4

David's SOS

For the Leader; upon the Nehiloth. A Psalm of David.

Give ear to my words, O LORD,
consider my meditation.
Hearken unto the voice of my cry, my King,
and my God;
For unto Thee do I pray.

O LORD, in the morning shalt Thou hear my voice;
In the morning will I order my prayer
unto Thee, and will look forward.
For Thou art not a God that hath pleasure
in wickedness;
Evil shall not sojourn with Thee.
The boasters shall not stand in Thy sight;
Thou hatest all workers of iniquity.
Thou destroyest them that speak falsehood;
The LORD abhorreth the man of blood
and of deceit.

But as for me, in the abundance of Thy
lovingkindness will I come into Thy house;
I will bow down toward Thy holy temple
in the fear of Thee.

O LORD, lead me in Thy righteousness because
of them that lie in wait for me;
Make Thy way straight before my face.
For there is no sincerity in their mouth;
Their inward part is a yawning gulf,
Their throat is an open sepulchre;
They make smooth their tongue.
Hold them guilty, O God,
Let them fall by their own counsels;
Cast them down in the multitude
of their transgressions;
For they have rebelled against Thee.

So shall all those that take refuge in Thee rejoice,
They shall ever shout for joy,
And Thou shalt shelter them;
Let them also that love Thy name exult in Thee.
For Thou dost bless the righteous;
O LORD, Thou dost encompass him
with favour as with a shield. (Psalm 5)

M ost people in the world experience some level of stress and anxiety. Parents bring a son or daughter into the world and often worry about the child's future. Pressures at work can be a source of daily stress. Financial burdens can steal peace. An illness can stir fear in the soul.

What do we do with stress and anxiety? The Bible was written by people who shared our human condition. They lived in a world full of hardship and uncertainty, as David expressed in Psalm 5.

This prayer of lament and petition was written for music, to be played on the pipes, or *chalil*. It is a piercing cry for God's protection during a time of severe anxiety. David's words provide an opportunity to see inside the heart and mind of someone who is worried and needing help.

David opens by saying that he prays "in the morning" (verse 4). At the beginning of his day, the king of Israel addresses God, who David trusts as his "King" (verse 3). He believes God hears his voice when he prays (verse 4). The first verses of the psalm reveal that David is transparent with God about his emotions. He says, "Consider my meditation" and "Hearken unto the voice of my cry."

Did this transparency help him? We can't know everything David felt, but at the end of the psalm he implies that he found "refuge" and even joy in God (verse 12). In verse 8, David says that he experiences God's abundant "lovingkindness," an indication that he doesn't feel alone in his hardships.

Also, in verses 9–10, David asks God to lead him in righteousness in the burdensome situations created by his foes. In the midst of opposition, David expresses his eagerness to avoid doing anything wrong that would defame God. Perhaps David is rising above his stress by not focusing on himself but on God's purposes.

This psalm reflects the struggles of a king who, like us, faces hardship and adversity. He is not immune from anguish and sadness. Yet, David takes all this to God, in whom he seeks protection.

PRAYER

Blessed are you, O Lord our God, King of the universe, who removes sleep from my eyes and slumber from my eyelids.

Blessed are you, O Lord our God, King of the universe, who has given us the Law of truth and has planted everlasting life in our midst.

Shema Yisrael Adonai Eloheinu, Adonai Echad.

And you shall love the Lord your God with all your heart, and with all your soul, and with all your might. And these words which I command you this day shall be upon your heart: and you shall teach them diligently to your children, and shall talk of them when you sit in your house, and when you walk by the way, and when you lie down, and when you rise up. And you shall bind them for a sign upon your hand, and they shall be for frontlets between your eyes. And you shall write them upon the doorposts of your house and upon your gates.

O my God, guard my tongue from evil, and my lips from speaking guile.

Let the words of my mouth and the meditation of my heart be acceptable before you, O Lord, my Rock and my Redeemer.

Through the Crucible to Peace

For the Leader; with string-music; on the Sheminith.
A Psalm of David.

O LORD, rebuke me not in Thine anger,
Neither chasten me in Thy wrath.
Be gracious unto me, O LORD, for I languish away;
Heal me, O LORD, for my bones are affrighted.
My soul also is sore affrighted;
And Thou, O LORD, how long?

Return, O LORD, deliver my soul;
Save me for Thy mercy's sake.
For in death there is no remembrance of Thee;
In the nether-world who will give Thee thanks?
I am weary with my groaning;
Every night make I my bed to swim;
I melt away my couch with my tears.

Mine eye is dimmed because of vexation;
  It waxeth old because of all mine adversaries.

Depart from me, all ye workers of iniquity;
  For the LORD hath heard the voice of my weeping.
The LORD hath heard my supplication;
  The LORD receiveth my prayer.
All mine enemies shall be ashamed and sore affrighted;
  They shall turn back, they shall
    be ashamed suddenly. (Psalm 6)

Humility is often equated with weakness and resignation. Being humble can seem like a recipe for failure in a competitive world. To succeed, people sometimes feel they have to barrel over anyone who gets in the way. However, Psalm 6 conveys a different perspective about humility, showing it to be a doorway to freedom and peace.

King David, writing in Psalm 6, conveys a deep brokenness and humility before God. In the first verses of the psalm, David appears to struggle with his conscience. He is concerned that God will "rebuke" him or "chasten" him.

Overcome with a guilty conscience, David tells God openly that his guilt is affecting him physically and emotionally. "I languish away," David says, adding that his "bones are affrighted" (verse 3). In this time of anguish, the psalm portrays a man who is seeking restoration and shalom (peace) with God. David cries out, "Be gracious unto me, O LORD" (verse 3) and "Return, O LORD, deliver my soul" (verse 5).

David also implies, in verse 7, that his struggles appear more difficult in the quiet of the night, when he reflects on his sins. The psalm doesn't specify the nature of his wrongdoing, but David weeps so much that his bed becomes soaked with tears.

Deeper still, David senses that God has turned away from him. For this reason he calls on God to "return" to him (verse 5). This distance from God might have caused him to sense the dark dread of death. In verse 6, he writes, "For in death there is no remembrance of Thee; in the netherworld who will give Thee thanks?" In this state of humble remorse, David calls on God to rescue him (verse 3).

The joy in the psalm emerges at the end. David announces, "The LORD hath heard the voice of my weeping. . . . The LORD receiveth my prayer" (verses 9–10). This can be seen as a demonstration of humility's restorative power. As David humbles himself and is transparent, he finds that God listens to him and forgives him.

The experience David so openly describes in Psalm 6 is conveyed by the meaning of the word *repentance*, or *teshuvah*, which describes a person who becomes troubled by wrongdoing and then, in humility, accepts responsibility. Psalm 6 can be seen as David's journey through a crucible until he finds peace and at-one-ment (atonement) with God. Forgiven by God, David is now free to move forward in life.

PRAYER

Our God and God of our fathers, let our prayer come before you; do not hide yourself from our supplication, for we are not arrogant and stiff-necked, that we should say before you, God and God of our fathers, we are righteous and have not sinned; but truly, we have sinned.

We have trespassed, we have been faithless, we have robbed, we have spoken basely, we have committed iniquity, we have cultivated unrighteousness, deliberately sinned presumptuous, we have extorted, we have forged lies, we have counseled evil, we have spoken falsely, we have scoffed, we have revolted, we have blasphemed, we have been rebellious, we have angered you, we have acted perversely, we have transgressed, we have persecuted, we have been stiff-necked, we have done wickedly, we have corrupted ourselves, we have committed abomination, we have gone astray, and we have led astray.

May it be your will, O Lord our God and God of our fathers, to forgive us for all our sins, to pardon us for all our iniquities, and to grant us remission for all our transgressions.

Facing Injustice

Shiggaion of David, which he sang unto the LORD,
concerning Cush a Benjamite.

O LORD my God, in Thee have I taken refuge;
  Save me from all them that pursue me, and deliver me;
Lest he tear my soul like a lion,
  Rending it in pieces, while there is none to deliver.

O LORD my God, if I have done this;
  If there be iniquity in my hands;
If I have requited him that did evil unto me,
  Or spoiled mine adversary unto emptiness;
Let the enemy pursue my soul, and overtake it,
  And tread my life down to the earth;
  Yea, let him lay my glory in the dust.

Selah

Arise, O LORD, in Thine anger,
  Lift up Thyself in indignation against mine adversaries;

Yea, awake for me at the judgment
which Thou hast commanded.
And let the congregation of the peoples
compass Thee about,
And over them return Thou on high.

O LORD, who ministerest judgment to the peoples,
Judge me, O LORD,
According to my righteousness, and according to
mine integrity that is in me.
Oh that a full measure of evil might
come upon the wicked,
And that Thou wouldest establish the righteous;
For the righteous God trieth the heart and reins.
My shield is with God,
Who saveth the upright in heart. . . .

He hath digged a pit, and hollowed it,
And is fallen into the ditch which he made.
His mischief shall return upon his own head,
And his violence shall come down
upon his own pate.
I will give thanks unto the LORD
according to His righteousness;
And will sing praise to the name of the
LORD Most High. (Psalm 7)

P salm 7 is laden with David's anguish and anger about the serious threat of his enemies. David compares his pursuers to ravenous predators: "Lest he tear my soul like a lion, rending it in pieces, while there is none to deliver" (verse 3).

It is helpful to understand the context of this psalm. As David gains prominence and power, a jealous King Saul pursues David, forcing him to flee and hide. But David responds by showing Saul mercy. First Samuel 24 describes an opportunity to kill Saul while Saul sleeps. Instead of taking justice into his own hands, David only cuts off the corner of Saul's garment.

David's mercy shows up again after the deaths of Saul and Jonathan. He writes a beautiful prayer of mourning: "Saul and Jonathan, the lovely and the pleasant . . . I am distressed for thee, my brother Jonathan; very pleasant hast thou been unto me" (2 Samuel 1:23–27). Despite the injustice of Saul, David still expresses love for him.

David's merciful response to his enemies also appears after he becomes king in Hebron. Saul's son Ish-bosheth makes war with David for seven years. However, when Ish-bosheth is murdered, David punishes those who killed him and gives him a proper burial (2 Samuel 4).

How, when faced with these injustices, was David able to avoid seeking revenge? It's possible that Psalm 7 sheds light on that question. In the psalm, David asks God to arise and vindicate him. David puts his trust in God to be the judge (verses 7–9).

As king, David might be within his rights to seek vengeance against those spreading sedition against him, but David chooses a different path. He calls upon God to avenge him. Rather than taking revenge, he trusts that his enemy will fall "into the ditch which he made" (verse 16) and that his enemy's schemes will backfire on him (verse 17). David does not take justice into his own hands.

Psalm 7 also portrays David, in the midst of these threats, trusting God for his own protection. Even at a terrible point in his life, David puts his life in God's care. He prays, "Oh that a full measure of evil might come upon the wicked, and that Thou wouldest establish the righteous; for the righteous God trieth the heart and reins. My shield is with God [*El Elyon*], Who saveth the upright in heart" (verses 10–11).

In this psalm, we find an opportunity to consider some powerful responses to injustice. Like David, may we find ways to avoid revenge and find peace.

PRAYER

True it is that you are indeed the Lord of your people, and a mighty King to plead their cause. True it is that you are indeed the first and the last. Beside you we have no King, Redeemer, and Savior. From Egypt you redeemed us, O Lord our God, and from the house of slavery you delivered us; all their firstborn you slayed, but your firstborn you redeemed; you divided the Red Sea, and drowned the proud; but you made the beloved to pass through, while the waters covered their adversaries, not one of whom was left. The beloved praised and extolled you, God, and offered hymns, songs, praises, blessings, and thanksgivings to the King and God who lives and endures; who is high and exalted, great and revered; who brings low the haughty and raises up the lowly, who leads forth the prisoners, delivers the meek, helps the poor, and answers his people when they cry to him; even praises to the Most High God, blessed is he, and ever to be blessed.

O Rock of Israel, arise to help and deliver Judah and Israel, according to your promise. Our Redeemer, the Lord of hosts is his name, the Holy One of Israel. Blessed are you, O Lord, who has redeemed Israel. Amen.

Celebrate the Victories

For the Leader; upon Muthlabben. A Psalm of David.

I will give thanks unto the LORD with my whole heart;
I will tell of all Thy marvellous works.
I will be glad and exult in Thee;
I will sing praise to Thy name, O Most High:

When mine enemies are turned back,
They stumble and perish at Thy presence;
For Thou hast maintained my right and my cause;
Thou sattest upon the throne as the righteous Judge.

Thou hast rebuked the nations,
Thou hast destroyed the wicked,
Thou hast blotted out their name for ever and ever.
O thou enemy, the waste places are come
to an end for ever;

And the cities which thou didst uproot,
Their very memorial is perished.

But the LORD is enthroned for ever;
He hath established His throne for judgment.
And He will judge the world in righteousness,
He will minister judgment to the
peoples with equity.

The LORD also will be a high tower for the oppressed,
A high tower in times of trouble;
And they that know Thy name will put their trust
in Thee;
For thou, LORD, hast not forsaken them
that seek Thee. (Psalm 9:1–11)

Victories are celebrated differently in different sports. Race car drivers spin donuts on the track, burning rubber in clouds of smoke. Baseball players run from the dugout and dogpile near the pitcher's mound. Cyclists who win the Tour de France spray champagne.

Celebration is a prominent part of the Bible too. For example, when Nehemiah's team finished building the wall around Jerusalem, a huge crowd and a choir gathered to celebrate. "And they offered great sacrifices that day and rejoiced, for God had made them rejoice with great joy;

the women and the children also rejoiced. And the joy of Jerusalem was heard far away" (Nehemiah 12:43, ESV).

Some of the Bible's authors celebrated by writing songs, poems, or prayers. Usually these writings give credit to God for helping people. This is evident in David's joyful prayer in Psalm 9. This psalm was later used for worship at the temple in Jerusalem, where it would have been sung by the Levites while the priests offered sacrifices in the courtyard. The prayer (combined with Psalm 10) is an acrostic—each stanza begins with a letter of the Hebrew alphabet, and they are arranged in alphabetical order.

According to Jewish tradition, this prayer is related to David's victory over Goliath and the Philistines (1 Samuel 17). But even if David was writing about some other experience, you might call the psalm one of David's victory laps.

In Psalm 9, David reminisces about everything that God has done for him. In verse 2 David praises God for his "marvelous works" (*niflotecha*). He gives credit to God, rather than himself. He speaks in awe of God's power to defeat the wicked and turn away seemingly invincible enemies (verse 4). In verses 8–9, he praises God for ruling the world with justice (*tzedek*).

Do you take time to celebrate the victories in your life—a newborn son or daughter, a job promotion, a child's acceptance into college, a wedding, a good health report? David's prayer in this psalm can be seen as a reminder to commemorate and appreciate the many good things in our lives.

PRAYER

Blessed are you, O Lord our God, King of the universe, O God, our Father, our King, our Mighty One, our Creator, our Redeemer, our Maker, our Holy One, the Holy One of Jacob, our Shepherd, the Shepherd of Israel, O King, who are kind and deals kindly with all. Day by day you have dealt kindly and do deal kindly, and will deal kindly with us. You have bestowed, you do bestow, and you will ever bestow benefits upon us, yielding us grace, loving-kindness, mercy and relief, deliverance and prosperity, blessing and salvation, consolation, sustenance and supports. You give mercy, life, peace, and all good: of no manner of good let us be in want. Amen.

Where Is God?

For the Leader. A Psalm of David.

How long, O LORD, wilt Thou forget me for ever?
How long wilt Thou hide Thy face from me?
How long shall I take counsel in my soul,
having sorrow in my heart by day?
How long shall mine enemy be exalted over me?
Behold Thou, and answer me, O LORD my God;
Lighten mine eyes, lest I sleep the sleep of death;
Lest mine enemy say: "I have prevailed against him";
Lest mine adversaries rejoice when I am moved.

But as for me, in Thy mercy do I trust;
My heart shall rejoice in Thy salvation.
I will sing unto the LORD,
Because He hath dealt bountifully
with me. (Psalm 13)

William Shakespeare, in his play *Hamlet*, shows Hamlet in a period of depression. He says:

I have of late—but wherefore I know not—lost all my mirth, foregone all custom of exercises; and—indeed— it goes so heavily with my disposition that this goodly frame, the earth, seems to me a sterile promontory.[2]

During difficult times of tragedy or sorrow, many people sense that God has turned away. It's as if he "hides his face" (*hester panim*).

This phrase appears in numerous books of the Bible. For example, after murdering his brother, Cain fears he will be hidden from God's face, or from God's presence (Genesis 4:14). Before Moses's death, God warns Moses that he will hide his face from the people of Israel after they forsake him and break their covenant with him (Deuteronomy 31:16–18). The prophets Isaiah (57:17) and Ezekiel (39:24) also use the phrase.

But this ominous, downcast experience is not always a consequence of wrongdoing in the Bible. In Psalm 13, there is no indication that David has committed a moral wrong, but he uses the phrase *hester panim* as he cries out to God with grief and fear. "How long, O LORD, wilt Thou forget me for ever? How long wilt Thou hide Thy face from me?" (verse 2). Has God forgotten him? Has God hidden his face? David seems to keenly miss the sense of God's presence as he wrestles with his sorrows and thoughts.

---

2   William Shakespeare, *Hamlet*, act 2, in Richard Winter, *The Roots of Sorrow* (Wipf and Stock Publishers, 1986), 18.

Added to his sense of God's absence, David expresses his fear that his enemies will prevail (verse 3). This vulnerability causes him to fear death (verse 4), and he sees his enemies rejoicing in his defeat (verse 5).

The structure of this powerful psalm makes it possible to see David moving through depression toward light and hope. Even in his sorrow and loneliness, David focuses on God's mercy for him (verse 6). And at the end of his prayer, we see David praising God for his salvation (*yeshua*).

Psalm 13 shows David, in difficult circumstances, trusting in God's unfailing love and looking for his salvation. David shows no signs in this prayer of giving up on God, even when he thinks God may have given up on him. In the end, his depression fades and his heart rejoices (verse 6).

Perhaps David's prayer can inspire us to see past the temporary, dark circumstances of life—when the world seems like "a sterile promontory"—and focus on lasting love and goodness.

PRAYER

Av ha-rachamim, Father who is full of compassion, please help to dispel the darkness that could overwhelm me. Do not hide your face from me! Grant me the gift of your presence, and the faith to believe in your goodness during difficult times. Help me to do your will. May I strengthen others in pain and despair, as you strengthen me. Amen.

My Refuge

Michtam of David.

Keep me, O God; for I have taken refuge in Thee.
I have said unto the LORD: "Thou art my Lord;
  I have no good but in Thee";
As for the holy that are in the earth,
  They are the excellent in whom is all my delight.
Let the idols of them be multiplied
    that make suit unto another;
  Their drink-offerings of blood will I not offer,
  Nor take their names upon my lips.
O LORD, the portion of mine inheritance
    and of my cup,
  Thou maintainest my lot.

The lines are fallen unto me in pleasant places;
  Yea, I have a goodly heritage.
I will bless the LORD, who hath given me counsel;
Yea, in the night seasons my reins instruct me.

I have set the LORD always before me;
Surely He is at my right hand, I shall not be moved.
Therefore my heart is glad, and my glory rejoiceth;
my flesh also dwelleth in safety;
For Thou wilt not abandon my soul to the nether-world;
Neither wilt Thou suffer Thy godly one to see the pit.
Thou makest me to know the path of life;
In Thy presence is fulness of joy,
In Thy right hand bliss for evermore. (Psalm 16)

The concept of God as refuge is prominent in Psalm 16. David expresses in the deepest terms his sense of security in God. He shares his belief that death—the "pit"—is facing him, but he finds joy and peace in the refuge of God. "He is at my right hand, I shall not be moved," David says (verse 8). In God's presence, he finds "fulness of joy" (verse 11).

This psalm of praise is called, in Hebrew, a *michtam*. There is some debate about the word's meaning. It could either describe a musical instrument or serve as an indicator of the prayer's importance (*michtam* has been translated as "golden" or "precious").

David proclaims his faith in God (verse 2) while he is surrounded by a culture of death and idolatry (verse 4). The world around him is heavy, dark, and oppressive. David alludes to the "drink-offerings of blood " (verse 4) of those who worship other gods. Although we can't be sure, it's possible that David was referring to the cult of Molech, which had rites of human sacrifice (Leviticus 18:21; 20:3–5; 2 Kings 23:10; Jeremiah 32:35).

Despite this, David expresses his certainty that God is the refuge for his soul, even in the face of death. For this reason he writes, "Thou wilt not abandon my soul to the nether-world" (verse 10). Although David knows he will someday die, these words indicate he does not believe the time has yet come for his body to enter the grave. David affirms how God has taught him "the path of life," which leads to "fulness of joy" in God's presence and the eternal "bliss" of his right hand (verse 11).

We, too, live in a world that includes death and sorrow, as well as joy and beauty. Regardless of the situation, David's psalm can serve to focus our attention on the need for physical and emotional refuge.

PRAYER

How precious is your lovingkindness, O God! And the children of men take refuge under the shadow of your wings. They sate themselves with the fatness of your house; and you give them to drink of the river of your pleasures. For with you is the fountain of life: in your light do we see light. O continue your lovingkindness unto them that know you, and your righteousness to the upright in heart.

Who's to Judge?

A Prayer of David.

Hear the right, O LORD, attend unto my cry;
*   Give ear unto my prayer from lips without deceit.*
Let my judgment come forth from Thy presence;
*   Let Thine eyes behold equity.*
Thou hast tried my heart, Thou hast visited it
*   in the night;*
*   Thou hast tested me, and Thou findest not*
*   That I had a thought which should not*
*   pass my mouth.*
As for the doings of men, by the word of Thy lips
*   I have kept me from the ways of the violent.*
My steps have held fast to Thy paths,
*   My feet have not slipped.*

As for me, I call upon Thee,
*   for Thou wilt answer me, O God;*
*   Incline Thine ear unto me, hear my speech.*

Make passing great Thy mercies, O Thou that savest
*   by Thy right hand*
* From assailants them that take refuge in Thee.*
Keep me as the apple of the eye,
*   Hide me in the shadow of Thy wings,*
From the wicked that oppress,
*   My deadly enemies, that compass me about.*
Their gross heart they have shut tight,
*   With their mouth they speak proudly.*
At our every step they have now encompassed us;
*   They set their eyes to cast us down to the earth.*
He is like a lion that is eager to tear in pieces,
*   And like a young lion lurking in secret places.*

Arise, O LORD, confront him, cast him down;
*   Deliver my soul from the wicked, by Thy sword;*
From men, by Thy hand, O LORD,
*   From men of the world, whose portion is*
*   in this life,*
*   And whose belly Thou fillest with Thy treasure;*
*   Who have children in plenty,*
*   And leave their abundance to their babes.*
As for me, I shall behold Thy face in righteousness;
*   I shall be satisfied, when I awake,*
*   with Thy likeness. (Psalm 17)*

How should we measure ourselves? In an era of social media, many people base their self-worth on how many people in a virtual community "like" them. Others view themselves through the lens of professional success. Who is the judge?

King David, as he writes in Psalm 17, seeks to base his life on God's standards for right and wrong, not on the world's perspectives. David writes: "Thou hast tested me, and Thou findest not . . . I have kept me from the ways of the violent. My steps have held fast to Thy paths, my feet have not slipped" (verses 3–5). David's words can help us consider the reference points by which we measure our lives and our culture.

David goes on to say in his prayer that it is God whom he seeks to please, not men: "Keep me as the apple of the eye" (verse 8). With these words, it's possible that David is seeking God's approval because he doesn't believe he can accurately judge himself, and because many people in the culture around him are pitiless, arrogant, wicked, and violent (verses 9–10).

Notice that David makes this request while he's in the midst of danger. He asks God to protect him "in the shadow of [God's] wings" (*kenafecha*) from men who would strike him dead with no pity or remorse (verses 8–10). He is surrounded and hunted (verse 11). It is as if a lion has his scent and will tear him into pieces if God does not rise and intervene (verses 12–14). But to confidently ask God for protection, David seems to feel the need for greater certainty about his moral standing before God, not based on his own perspective of himself, but based on God's righteous judgment.

David's prayer can help us consider how we measure ourselves, especially as we deal with different struggles in life. As this psalm shows, David believed that he needed God to be his measure. This relationship appears to have helped him avoid rationalizing wrong attitudes and behaviors. Perhaps God also helped him break free from false guilt, as well as the inaccurate standards of the world around him.

In the Jewish tradition, David's thoughts in Psalm 17 resonate with the *Malchuyot* (kingliness) prayer from the High Holy Days Liturgy: "God is the incomparable King of the Universe. The destiny of humanity is to come to this realization. Whereas human kings rule in accordance with the principle of 'might makes right,' God is the Holy King, Who is, at the same time, beyond comparison in His power. . . . He is also the Father of the orphan and the Judge of the widow, Who is always on the side of the powerless."

Dayan HaEmet, True Judge, search my soul. Help me to fix my flaws and correct my errors, so that my actions may be pleasing in your sight. Give me the wisdom to forgive myself for my guilt over what I cannot control. Remove from me sorrow and sighing, and reign over us, you alone, O Lord, with kindness and compassion, with righteousness and justice. Blessed are you, Lord, king who loves righteousness and justice. Like David, I ask that you vindicate my life and protect me from causeless hatred. May my words and deeds be pleasing to you, my judge and comforter. *Baruch Atah Adonai,* praised are you, Lord, king who loves righteousness and justice. Amen.

11

A Military Blessing

For the Leader. A Psalm of David.

The LORD answer thee in the day of trouble;
The name of the God of Jacob set thee up on high;
Send forth thy help from the sanctuary,
And support thee out of Zion;
Receive the memorial of all thy meal-offerings,
And accept the fat of thy burnt-sacrifice;

Selah

Grant thee according to thine own heart,
And fulfil all thy counsel.
We will shout for joy in thy victory,
And in the name of our God
we will set up our standards;
The LORD fulfil all thy petitions.

Now know I that the LORD saveth His anointed;
He will answer him from His holy heaven

With the mighty acts of His saving right hand.
Some trust in chariots, and some in horses;
    But we will make mention of the
        name of the LORD our God.
They are bowed down and fallen;
    But we are risen, and stand upright.
Save, LORD;
    Let the King answer us in the day
        that we call. (Psalm 20)

T his psalm is a blessing and prayer for victory, most
    likely as David and his army march to war. David
probably wrote this psalm to bless his men who were
about to fight. At the time this psalm was written, kings
often joined their armies in battle. In the Hebrew Bible,
David is a warrior-king who is often seen fighting along
with his soldiers. The final verse of the psalm is a direct
request for God to save the king.

In addition to a plea for protection, it is possible that
David is seeking confirmation from God that the battle
will be just and moral. In verse 3, he asks God to send
victory from "the sanctuary" (*mi-kodesh*, meaning "from
holiness"). In the Jewish tradition, this is a reference to
the temple. When David asks for support from the sanctuary, it's possible that he realizes the cause is futile if it is
not holy and just in God's eyes.

David then changes his tone and turns the prayer into a statement of faith. He says he knows that without God's help they will fail. He states that victory happens not because of weaponry but because of "the mighty acts of [God's] saving right hand" (verse 7). This is similar to the words in Zechariah 4:6: "'Not by might nor by power, but by my Spirit,' says the Lord Almighty" (NIV).

As we consider this psalm, we can remember to pray for the protection of those who are in battle, and to pray for the nation's leaders, that they might make wise and moral decisions about wars and battles.

For this reason, most synagogues include prayers for whichever country they happen to be in and for the protection of the State of Israel in Sabbath liturgy. All of us can pray for our military, our elected leaders, and the welfare of our people.

PRAYER FOR THE GOVERNMENT

He who gives salvation to kings and dominion unto princes, whose kingdom is an everlasting kingdom, who delivered his servant David from the hurtful sword, who makes a way in the sea and a path in the mighty waters, may he bless, guard, protect, and help, exalt, magnify, and highly aggrandize the constituted officers of this government.

May the supreme King of kings in his mercy preserve them in life and deliver them from all trouble and hurt. May the supreme King of kings in his mercy exalt them and raise them on high, and grant them a long and prosperous rule. May the supreme King of kings in his mercy inspire them and all their counselors and officers with benevolence toward us, and all Israel. In their days and in ours may Judah be saved and Israel dwell securely; and may the redeemer come unto Zion. O that this may be his will, and let us say, Amen.

Grief and Hope

For the Leader; upon Aijeleth ha-Shanar. A Psalm of David.

My God, my God, why hast Thou forsaken me,
And art far from my help at the words of my cry?
O my God, I call by day, but Thou answerest not;
And at night, and there is no surcease for me.
Yet Thou art holy,
O Thou that art enthroned upon the praises of Israel.
In Thee did our fathers trust;
They trusted, and Thou didst deliver them.
Unto Thee they cried, and escaped;
In Thee did they trust, and were not ashamed.
But I am a worm, and no man;
A reproach of men, and despised of the people.
All they that see me laugh me to scorn;
They shoot out the lip, they shake the head:
"Let him commit himself unto the LORD!
let Him rescue him;
Let Him deliver him, seeing He delighteth in him."...

I will declare Thy name unto my brethren;
  In the midst of the congregation will I praise Thee.
"Ye that fear the LORD, praise Him;
  All ye the seed of Jacob, glorify Him;
  And stand in awe of Him, all ye the seed of Israel.
For He hath not despised nor abhorred
    the lowliness of the poor;
  Neither hath He hid His face from him;
  But when he cried unto Him, He heard."
From Thee cometh my praise in the great congregation;
  I will pay my vows before them that fear Him.
Let the humble eat and be satisfied;
  Let them praise the LORD that seek after Him;
    May your heart be quickened for ever!
All the ends of the earth shall remember
    and turn unto the LORD;
  And all the kindreds of the nations
    shall worship before Thee.
For the kingdom is the LORD's;
  And He is the ruler over the nations.
All the fat ones of the earth shall eat and worship;
  All they that go down to the dust shall kneel before Him,
  Even he that cannot keep his soul alive.
A seed shall serve him;
  It shall be told of the LORD unto the next generation.
They shall come and shall declare His righteousness
  Unto a people that shall be born, that He hath
    done it. (Psalm 22)

David's prayer begins with the raw and honest confession that he is heartsick and abandoned, feeling that there is no one to heal him, not even God, who has seemingly forsaken him (verse 2). He cries from the innermost depths of his soul, yet God is silent (verse 3). Day and night, his pleas ascend to heaven, and it seems they are not heard.

Many people can relate to David's grief, or what some theologians call the "dark night of the soul." Hardships in life—losing a child to an illness, a divorce, a period of unemployment—can often create conditions for depression. This psalm looks at that type of suffering square in the face. And without empty platitudes, David concludes his prayer in a place of meaning and hope.

In the midst of his despondent moment, David contrasts his situation to that of his ancestors, the Israelites whom God delivered from slavery in Egypt. God heard them and rescued them (verses 5–6; see Exodus 3:7). Yet God seems ambivalent to David's prayers. Perhaps David is asking God, "Why did you help them, but not me?" With no immediate answer to that question, it's likely that he feels even more alone.

In addition to feeling abandoned, David says he is scorned, despised, and mocked (verses 7–8). People in his circle of relationships make fun of him, saying that if he is so beloved of God, then God should save him (verse 9).

At the end of his prayer, David seems to have come to a place of greater hope and light. In acknowledging

God's goodness, David says that God has heard his cries (verse 25) and that the "humble" will "eat and be satisfied" (verse 27). David is able to see hope in God's work into the next generations (verses 31–32).

Based on this psalm's hopeful conclusion, we can see that David's experience with abandonment and depression is temporary. The darkness passes and new horizons come into view. There might be times in life when we also feel abandoned and full of grief. When we are ill, or when there has been a death in the family, we might sense that there is no response from God. Although we don't know how long it took, David finds his condition to be momentary. The psalm invites us to consider David's belief that God does answer and will act (verse 27).

In Isaiah we read, " 'Do not be afraid, you worm Jacob, little Israel, do not fear, for I myself will help you,' declares the LORD, your Redeemer, the Holy One of Israel" (41:14, NIV). God guided and supported Abraham, Isaac, and Jacob even in times of dread. These biblical texts also invite us to not lose hope.

PRAYER

We beseech you, O gracious and merciful King, remember and give heed to the covenant between the pieces (with Abraham), and let the binding (upon the altar) of (Isaac) an only son appear before you, to the welfare of Israel. Our Father, our King, be gracious unto us and answer us, for we are called by your great name. You, who do wondrous things at all times, deal with us according to your loving-kindness. O gracious and merciful Being, look, and answer us in time of trouble, for salvation is yours, O Lord. Our Father, our King, our Refuge, deal not with us according to the evil of our doings. Remember, O Lord, your tender mercies and loving-kindnesses; save us according to your abundant goodness, and have pity upon us, we beseech you, for we have no other God beside you, our Rock. And David said unto Gad, I am troubled exceedingly; let us fall, I pray, into the hand of the Lord, for his mercies are many; but let me not fall into the hand of humans. Blessed are you, O Lord, Redeemer of Israel. Amen.

Satisfaction with the Shepherd

A Psalm of David.

The LORD is my shepherd; I shall not want.
He maketh me to lie down in green pastures;
He leadeth me beside the still waters.
He restoreth my soul;
He guideth me in straight paths
for His name's sake.
Yea, though I walk through the valley
of the shadow of death,
I will fear no evil, for Thou art with me;
Thy rod and Thy staff, they comfort me.
Thou preparest a table before me
in the presence of mine enemies;
Thou hast anointed my head with oil;
my cup runneth over.

Surely goodness and mercy shall follow me
all the days of my life;
And I shall dwell in the house of the LORD
for ever. (Psalm 23)

M any of us seldom feel satisfied. We want more time. We want more money. We want success. We want to be thinner, taller, stronger, younger. Often we don't even know *what* we want; we just know we want differently than what we have. This constant sense of dissatisfaction can feed a life with worry, stress, fear, and restlessness. In this well-known prayer, David declares he wants for nothing because God is his shepherd.

David spent his youth in the fields tending his father's sheep (1 Samuel 16:10–11), until God "took him from the sheepfolds" to rule over Israel (Psalm 78:70–72). In 2 Samuel 5:2 "shepherd" is used as a metaphor for a king. Psalm 80:1 describes God as the "Shepherd of Israel." Isaiah says of God, "He will tend his flock like a shepherd; he will gather the lambs in his arms; he will carry them in his bosom, and gently lead those that are with young" (Isaiah 40:11, ESV).

Sheep are panicky, prone to wander, defenseless, and completely dependent. In Psalm 23 David appears to humbly rejoice at being a sheep in his shepherd's flock.

He articulates that God is concerned with his welfare and will meet all his needs.

In saying, "He maketh me to lie down" (verse 2), David most likely isn't implying that God forces him to take a nap, as parents may have to do for a cranky toddler. Instead, David's words point to God as his source of much-needed rest. Sheep are fearful animals and cannot lie down unless they feel completely safe. David communicates that he feels so secure in his shepherd's abundant care that he can rest and receive nourishment in God's green pastures (Ezekiel 34:14).

David trusts his shepherd to lead him "beside the still waters" (verse 2) that soothe, rather than raging rapids that cause sheep to feel rushed and endangered. David expresses a willingness to follow God, convinced that his shepherd will guide him on the straightest path to refreshment and restoration. As a shepherd, God restores David's "soul" (verse 3). In another of David's prayers, he states that the perfect "law of the Lord" works this great revival of his soul (Psalm 19:8).

As a young shepherd, David may have led his father's sheep through narrow ravines where the steep, surrounding slopes cast dark shadows and provided hiding places for predators. As a king, David experienced times of extreme danger, such as when he hid in dark caves from those who sought to kill him (1 Samuel 22, 24). Despite all of life's hardships and heartaches, David makes the decision to "fear no evil" (verse 4). He gains comfort in knowing that the shepherd's "rod" and "staff" will protect, guide, and rescue him (verse 4).

David transitions from rejoicing over how God, his shepherd, cares for him to marveling at how God, his host, welcomes him. In David's Israelite culture, eating a meal with others signified acceptance and relationship. The image of God setting out "a table" before David in the presence of his enemies (verse 5) suggests God's care for him involves not just protecting him from his enemies but also honoring him as his enemies look on.

In this psalm, David doesn't seem concerned about enemies pursuing him. Instead, he states that God's "goodness" and his "mercy"—*chesed,* God's steadfast, loyal love—will stay with him throughout all his life (verse 6). Because of this confidence in God's enduring love, David concludes he will "dwell in the house of the LORD for ever" (verse 6). In Psalm 27:4, David reveals his heartfelt desire to live in the presence of God: "One thing have I asked of the LORD, that will I seek after: that I may dwell in the house of the LORD all the days of my life, to gaze upon the beauty of the LORD" (ESV).

Like David, who was often surrounded by physical enemies and faced with discouragement, we live through moments of trials in our lives. During these times it can be easy to allow dissatisfaction to plague our lives with worry and stress. Perhaps we can receive encouragement from David's words in Psalm 23 as he expresses his contentment with God's provision and protection for him.

Behold, God is my salvation; I will trust, and will not be afraid: for the Lord is my strength and song, and he is become my salvation. Therefore with joy shall you draw water out of the wells of salvation. Salvation belongs to the Lord: your blessing be upon your people. (Selah.) The Lord of hosts is with us; the God of Jacob is our refuge. (Selah.) The Jews had light and joy and gladness and honor. So be it with us. I will lift the cup of salvation, and call upon the name of the Lord.

Seeking the Path of God

[A Psalm] of David.

Unto Thee, O LORD, do I lift up my soul.

ב

O my God, in Thee have I trusted,
let me not be ashamed;
Let not mine enemies triumph over me.

ג

Yea, none that wait for Thee shall be ashamed;
They shall be ashamed that deal treacherously
without cause.

ז

Show me Thy ways, O LORD;
teach me Thy paths.

Guide me in Thy truth, and teach me;
For Thou art the God of my salvation;
For Thee do I wait all the day.

ז

Remember, O LORD, Thy compassions and Thy mercies;
For they have been from of old.

ח

Remember not the sins of my youth, nor
my transgressions;
According to Thy mercy remember Thou me,
For Thy goodness' sake, O LORD.

ט

Good and upright is the LORD;
Therefore doth He instruct sinners in the way.

י

He guideth the humble in justice;
And He teacheth the humble His way.

כ

All the paths of the LORD are mercy and truth
Unto such as keep His covenant
and His testimonies. (Psalm 25:1–10)

Young people taking their first steps on the staircase of professional life often experience a sense of adventure and independence, while their parents hope they have given them the wisdom they need to thrive.

Although there is uncertainty regarding the context of this prayer, Psalm 25 could be one of David's teachings to prepare Solomon for kingship. This viewpoint is based on the psalm's thematic similarities to 1 Kings 2, in which the author recounts David's effort to pass his reign to Solomon. In that biblical text, David says to Solomon, "So be strong, act like a man, and observe what the LORD your God requires: Walk in obedience to him, and keep his decrees and commands, his laws and regulations, as written in the Law of Moses. Do this so that you may prosper in all you do and wherever you go" (1 Kings 2:2–3, NIV).

Psalm 25 may also have been used to teach children. It is written as an acrostic with a letter of the Hebrew alphabet sequentially leading each line of the prayer. This would have made it easy for young people to memorize.

Moreover, there are indications that David wants to be honest about his own experiences as a young person. Perhaps for this reason, he mentions "the sins of [his] youth" and his "transgressions" (verse 7). In terms of parent-child relationships, David's model of transparency might help parents today consider ways to instruct children while maintaining strong rapport.

In verse 4, David includes the analogy of a path, a powerful image for young people starting out on a journey.

David says he seeks the path of God; he desires to live in such a way that his deeds and words are pleasing to God in whom he trusts (verses 4–5). *Derech* (a "path") in Hebrew is also a way of life.

On this path, David acknowledges God as a faithful guide who benevolently leads his people (verse 8) even though they are imperfect. In many ways, David's assertion can serve as a comfort to young people, giving them peace and courage to step into the unknowns of life. As David states, a requirement for following God's leading is humility. God guides "the humble in justice" (verse 9), and his paths are secured by his "mercy and truth" (verse 10).

It is interesting to observe this psalm's simplicity. David's teaching reduces life's success to foundational elements. In this simplicity, the psalm's message is affirmed by the prophet Micah's counsel: "He has shown you, O mortal, what is good. And what does the LORD require of you? To act justly and to love mercy and to walk humbly with your God" (Micah 6:8, NIV).

David indicates that even in times of distress we can look to God and keep his commandments. The psalm doesn't whitewash the fact that life is full of trials (verses 16–18). But it teaches that God will show us forgiveness, mercy, love, and truth. According to David, God is steadfast, faithful, reliable, and good.

As young people embrace their independence, they—and their parents—can learn from David's prayer and take comfort in God's presence. They can also find comfort in David's words in Psalm 25:14: "The friendship of the Lord is for those who fear him" (ESV).

Rumor Has It

[A Psalm] of David.

Judge me, O LORD, for I have walked in mine integrity,
    And I have trusted in the LORD without wavering.
Examine me, O LORD, and try me;
    Test my reins and my heart.
For Thy mercy is before mine eyes;
    And I have walked in Thy truth.
I have not sat with men of falsehood;
    Neither will I go in with dissemblers.
I hate the gathering of evil doers,
    And will not sit with the wicked.
I will wash my hands in innocency;
    So will I compass Thine altar, O LORD,
That I may make the voice of thanksgiving to be heard,
    And tell of all Thy wondrous works.

LORD, I love the habitation of Thy house,
    And the place where Thy glory dwelleth.

Gather not my soul with sinners,
  Nor my life with men of blood;
In whose hands is craftiness,
  And their right hand is full of bribes.
But as for me, I will walk in mine integrity;
  Redeem me, and be gracious unto me.
My foot standeth in an even place;
  In the congregations will I bless the LORD. (Psalm 26)

Rumors and gossip have a long and destructive history. Now, with the onset of social media, new avenues of defamatory bullying have become wide open. Although not living in our e-world, David endured character assassination, as we see in Psalm 26.

In this psalm, we read how David has fallen prey to what in Hebrew is called *lashon hara*—the "evil tongue," which is a metaphor for *gossip* or *rumor*. He responds to this injustice by calling upon God in a plea for God to vindicate him.

There are several possible contexts of his life for which David wrote this psalm. Was it during the time when Saul sought to kill him (1 Samuel 20–23)? Or when his son Absalom rebelled against him (2 Samuel 15)? Or perhaps it was later, when Adonijah sought to usurp Solomon's reign (1 Kings 1:5, 11–14).

Whatever the context, David begins his prayer by pleading for vindication over those who would challenge his reputation (verse 1). David asks God to search his heart and probe his life, so that he is not justified by his opinion of himself but by God's righteous judgment (verse 2).

In the next few verses, David explains the ways he has kept himself from wrongdoing. From these statements, we might conclude people are accusing him of lying, consorting with hypocrites, and collaborating with evildoers. These false rumors seem to be spreading. But David makes it clear that he wants nothing to do with any of that (verse 5). Instead, David washes his hands and goes before the altar of God (verse 6).

In the Jewish tradition, washing hands before entering the temple was a ritual of purification before "meeting" with God. David is seeking the presence of God (verse 8) in the midst of severe opposition (verse 9).

In these verses, we can see David avoiding the corrupt ways of the world in which he lives (verses 10–11). Instead, he sees greater value in filling his soul by praying in the dwelling place of God (verses 7–8). In the last two verses of the psalm, David pleads with God to redeem him and to lead him on the level path of the *mitzvot* (commandments). He promises to praise God openly in his court.

Many believe David's son Solomon wrote the following words in the book of Proverbs warning against gossip: "A perverse person stirs up conflict, and a gossip separates close friends" (16:28, NIV). Perhaps David's desire voiced in his prayer to "walk in . . . integrity" (Psalm 26:11) and keep himself "in an even place" (verse 12) compelled him to teach Solomon about the importance of avoiding the wickedness of gossip.

This prayer of David challenges us to examine our own speech. It can be seen as a call to practice self-control in what we say and write, and as a reminder that everything we say, publicly and privately, has consequences. We can avoid being the cause of suffering if we commit ourselves to the pursuit of love and kindness in our speech. Similarly, Job stated, "My lips will not say anything wicked, and my tongue will not utter lies" (Job 27:4).

PRAYER

My God! Guard my tongue from evil and my lips from speaking deceit; and to those who curse me, let my soul be silent. Yes, let my soul be unto all as the dust. Open my heart to your Law, and let my soul pursue your commandments. If any design evil against me, speedily make their counsel of none effect, and frustrate their designs. Do it for the sake of your name; do it for the sake of your right hand; do it for the sake of your holiness; do it for the sake of your Law. In order that your beloved ones may be delivered, O save with your right hand, and answer me. Let the words of my mouth and the meditation of my heart be acceptable before you, O Lord, my Rock and my Redeemer. He who makes peace in his high places, may he make peace for us and for all Israel. Amen.

Overcoming Fear

[A Psalm] of David.

The LORD is my light and my salvation;
whom shall I fear?
The LORD is the stronghold of my life;
of whom shall I be afraid?
When evil-doers came upon me to eat up my flesh,
Even mine adversaries and my foes,
they stumbled and fell.
Though a host should encamp against me,
My heart shall not fear;
Though war should rise up against me,
Even then will I be confident.

One thing have I asked of the LORD,
that will I seek after:
That I may dwell in the house of the
LORD all the days of my life,
To behold the graciousness of the LORD,

and to visit early in His temple.
For He concealeth me in His pavilion in the day of evil;
He hideth me in the covert of His tent;
He lifteth me up upon a rock.
And now shall my head be lifted up above
mine enemies round about me;
And I will offer in His tabernacle
sacrifices with trumpet-sound;
I will sing, yea, I will sing praises unto the LORD.

Hear, O LORD, when I call with my voice,
And be gracious unto me, and answer me.
In Thy behalf my heart hath said: "Seek ye My face";
Thy face, LORD, will I seek.
Hide not Thy face far from me;
Put not Thy servant away in anger;
Thou hast been my help;
Cast me not off, neither forsake me,
O God of my salvation.
For though my father and my mother have forsaken me,
The LORD will take me up.

Teach me Thy way, O LORD;
And lead me in an even path,
Because of them that lie in wait for me.
Deliver me not over unto the will of mine adversaries;
For false witnesses are risen up against me,
and such as breathe out violence.

If I had not believed to look upon the
goodness of the LORD
In the land of the living!—
Wait on the LORD;
Be strong, and let thy heart take courage;
Yea, wait thou for the LORD. (Psalm 27)

J. R. R. Tolkien, in his trilogy The Lord of the Rings, often places his characters in ominous battles against evil enemies and under seemingly insurmountable opposition. Many of the characters, especially the hobbits, are physically small beings who love peace and comfort— they are not typical warriors. But Tolkien places these outwardly weak creatures in fearful situations that demand remarkable courage.

In the third book, *The Return of the King*, a dark evil spreads across the land. A soldier named Beregond describes the situation to Pippin, a hobbit: "Yes, the shadow of doom . . . Night comes. The very warmth of my blood seems stolen away."[3]

Pippin remembers that the good and powerful wizard, Gandalf, is present. He responds by saying: "No, my heart will not yet despair. Gandalf fell and has returned

3   J. R. R. Tolkien, *The Return of the King* (New York: Ballantine Books, 1965), 26.

and is with us. We may stand, if only on one leg, or at least be left still upon our knees."[4]

Such great stories echo the courage we find in Psalm 27. Here David expresses victory over his inner struggle with fear. David starts the psalm with a declaration of courage: "The LORD is my light and my salvation; whom shall I fear? The LORD is the stronghold of my life; of whom shall I be afraid?"

In this praise, David declares that his relationship with God, his light and strength, is the anchor of his life (verse 1). David has nothing to fear because God can deliver him from all evil (verses 1–2). Like a fortress, God protects David with his love even in the face of evil men and war (verses 2–3). His heart is not troubled; he has no anxiety because he has confidence in God (verse 3).

David's greatest joy is to experience God's presence—in God's holy place—every day (verse 4). Dwelling with God is directly connected to David's sense of security and courage. In the Jewish tradition, dwelling with God—and following his path—is a way of life. No wonder David pleads with God to continue as his ever-present help (verse 9). David does not want to be overcome by the schemes of his oppressors (verse 12).

In the midst of ominous threats, David finds comfort and courage in his relationship with God. In verse 14, David exhorts his readers: "Wait on the LORD; be strong, and let thy heart take courage; yea, wait thou for the LORD."

---

4   Ibid.

In many Jewish liturgical practices, this psalm is recited twice a day between Rosh Hashanah and Yom Kippur. Rosh Hashanah and Yom Kippur are days of judgment, and this psalm is recited to take courage in God's mercy.

Psalm 27 leads us to reflect on what role fear plays in our lives. Are we able, like David, to live courageously in the face of those fears? Perhaps, like David, we can say, "The LORD is my light and my salvation; whom shall I fear?"

PRAYER

Avinu Malkeinu, our Father our and King, bring us closer to you. Be merciful in your judgment of me, and help me to hear the gentle whisper of your presence speaking to my soul. May I, like David, rejoice in your goodness during the days of my life and be blessed with your love forever. Amen.

Hoping for Judgment

[A Psalm] of David.

Unto thee, O LORD, do I call;
My Rock, be not Thou deaf unto me;
Lest, if Thou be silent unto me,
I become like them that go down into the pit.
Hear the voice of my supplications,
when I cry unto Thee,
When I lift up my hands toward
Thy holy Sanctuary.

Draw me not away with the wicked,
And with the workers of iniquity;
Who speak peace with their neighbours,
But evil is in their hearts.
Give them according to their deeds, and according
to the evil of their endeavours;

Give them after the work of their hands;
Render to them their desert.
Because they give no heed to the works of the LORD,
Nor to the operation of His hands;
He will break them down and not build them up.

Blessed be the LORD,
Because He hath heard the voice of my supplications.
The LORD is my strength and my shield,
In Him hath my heart trusted, And I am helped;
Therefore my heart greatly rejoiceth,
And with my song will I praise Him.

The LORD is a strength unto them;
And He is a stronghold of salvation to His anointed.
Save Thy people, and bless Thine inheritance;
And tend them, and carry them for ever. (Psalm 28)

N o nation has perfect justice. Many systems of so-called justice are completely dysfunctional where victims of crime or injustice have no recourse. There is no fair judge who will hear their case or trustworthy lawyer to defend them. Without a fair system of justice, they must cope with personal loss and unresolved anger.

In Psalm 28 David makes a passionate plea for justice. He calls on God to pay evildoers "according to their deeds, and . . . render to them their desert" (verse 4). He raises the issue of reward and punishment (*sachar veonesh*) and wants to see the punishment fit the crime for the wicked due to "the evil of their endeavours" (verse 4). David sees God's judgment as a form of rescue and salvation from evil.

Often maligned and threatened, David asks God to punish those who are wicked, those who harbor "evil . . . in their hearts" (verse 3). Facing some real threat, he fears he could become like those who "go down into the pit" (verse 1)—namely, die—without God's hand of justice.

Although we can't be certain about what prompted David to write the psalm, his life is plagued by enemies who seek to destroy him and his reign as Israel's king. Some of his own sons, such as Absalom (2 Samuel 15), rebel against David, and the tribe of Benjamin never forgives him for the loss of royal privilege.

Whatever the circumstances motivating this prayer in Psalm 28, David acknowledges his complete dependence on God (verse 1). David stands in God's holy place and lifts his hands in supplication, pouring out his soul to God (verse 2). He asks for mercy and for God to intervene on his behalf.

Although we often don't like to think of God as a judge who metes out punishment, David boldly asks for the wicked to be punished (verses 3–4). He even asks God to tear them down, never to be rebuilt (verse 5). Perhaps David's sentiments are best understood by those who have suffered as victims of crime or oppression.

David's prayer ends with an appeal for those he governs, the people of Israel: "Save Thy people, and bless Thine inheritance" (verse 9). This could indicate that the injustice is impacting not just David but also his nation. If that is the case, we can understand why his call for God's justice is so fervent.

The fact that David seeks God's help and justice can be seen as David's way of not taking justice into his own hands. In his pain, David asks God to fulfill the role of judge. By trusting God to act as judge, David avoids planning his own revenge, which can spiral out of control. There is no guarantee of God's defense, but this prayer is already a blessing to David.

Reading Psalm 28:6, we see that David's trust in God pays off. He announces that God has heard his prayer for mercy. He has trusted God, and God has helped him. The result for David is joy and thankfulness (verse 7).

It is not clear in the psalm whether God brought judgment to David's oppressors at this time. What we know from the psalm is that, according to David, God gave him protection and strength (verses 6–7). David's experience is similar to what the prophet Isaiah wrote in Isaiah 58:9: "Then shall you call, and the LORD will answer: you shall cry, and he will say, 'Here I am'" (ESV).

Even in our personal relationships we often offend one another in small or serious ways. Feelings of injustice can cause anger and division. Psalm 28 can help us assess how we might respond to these injustices (severe or minor) and hopefully prevent ongoing conflict.

PRAYER

Blessed be the true Judge . . . for his judgment is true, and his eye discerns all things, and he awards unto man his reckoning and his sentence, and all must render acknowledgment unto him. We know, O Lord, that your judgment is righteous: you are justified when you speak, and pure when you judge, and it is not for us to murmur at your method of judging; you are just, O Lord, and your judgments are righteous. O true and righteous Judge! Blessed be the true Judge, all whose judgments are righteous and true. The soul of every living thing is in your hand; your right hand is full of righteousness.

Praise for Spiritual Healing

A Psalm; a Song at the Dedication of the House; of David.

> *I will extol thee, O LORD, for Thou hast raised me up,*
> > *And hast not suffered mine enemies*
> > > *to rejoice over me.*
> *O LORD my God,*
> > *I cried unto Thee, and Thou didst heal me;*
> *O LORD, Thou broughtest up my soul*
> > *from the nether-world;*
> > *Thou didst kept me alive, that I should*
> > > *not go down to the pit.*
> *Sing praise unto the LORD, O ye His godly ones,*
> > *And give thanks to His holy name.*
> *For His anger is but for a moment, His*
> > > *favour is for a life-time;*
> > *Weeping may tarry for the night,*
> > *But joy cometh in the morning.*

Now I had said in my security:
*   "I shall never be moved."*
Thou hadst established, O Lord, in Thy favour
*   my mountain as a stronghold—*
*   Thou didst hide Thy face; I was affrighted.*
Unto Thee, O Lord, did I call,
*   And unto the Lord I made supplication:*
"What profit is there in my blood, when
*   I go down to the pit?*
*   Shall the dust praise Thee? Shall*
*   it declare Thy truth?*
Hear, O Lord, and be gracious unto me;
*   Lord, be Thou my helper."*

Thou didst turn for me my mourning into dancing;
*   Thou didst loose my sackcloth, and*
*   gird me with gladness;*
So that my glory may sing praise to
*   Thee, and not be silent;*
*   O Lord my God, I will give thanks*
*   unto Thee for ever. (Psalm 30)*

There is perhaps no better feeling of relief than to receive word from a doctor that a serious illness has been overcome. In a similar way, people who overcome periods of deep sorrow, temptation, or sin experience relief when their suffering eases. The storm passes, the dark clouds lift, and joy breaks through. This prayer is a proclamation of victory and salvation from sin and sorrow.

According to the first verses of the psalm, David appears to be sorrowful to the point of death. He tells God, "Thou didst kept me alive, that I should not go down to the pit" (verse 4). God heals his malady and his life is spared (verse 3). Therefore, David gives thanks to God for giving him victory over whatever has caused him to suffer. "I will extol thee, O LORD, for Thou hast raised me up, and hast not suffered mine enemies to rejoice over me" (verse 2). He is saved from "the nether-world" (verse 4), or *Sheol*—a Hebrew word that conveys the grave or death.

Having overcome his period of anguish—after apparently receiving God's forgiveness—David breaks into celebration. He calls upon the faithful to sing and praise the name of God for his victory (verse 5). However, for the sake of others, he explains the malady that had such an impact on his spirit when he felt as though God had hidden his face from him (*hester panim*).

In this particular instance, the "illness" appears to be self-inflicted. David confesses, "Now I had said in my security: 'I shall never be moved' " (verse7). This pride resulted in God hiding his face from David. In this broken relationship, David realizes his hubris deserves death. Why should God support a king who is completely boastful? Once he realizes the gravity of his arrogance, David marshals three reasons why God should spare his life.

Feeling alone and abandoned, his weeping and pleas for mercy fill the night (verse 6). In his fear and repentance, David argues with God. In verse 10 he seeks to preserve his physical health. If he dies, David asks, how can he praise God? This argument has merit only if God knows him as one who praises. We know from the Psalms themselves that David has a record of offering God praise in spite of this aberration.

David offers God a second reason to spare his life. "Shall the dust . . . declare Thy truth?" (verse 10). Again, God can spare David's life because of David's reputation of declaring God's faithfulness.

Finally, David simply asks God, "What profit is there in my blood?" (verse 10). It is not as if David is afraid of dying, for Psalm 23:4 asserts, "Yea, though I walk through the valley of the shadow of death, I will fear no evil." But David believes at this moment his death would be untimely—he would no longer be useful to God in this life. Again, this argument only has merit to the extent that David has been useful to God in the past.

Although we can't be sure that God restores David because of these arguments, David claims in the psalm that God hears him and grants healing. Knowing the danger of death has passed, David celebrates: "Thou didst turn for me my mourning into dancing . . . and gird me with gladness; so that my glory may sing praise to Thee, and not be silent; O LORD my God, I will give thanks unto Thee for ever" (verses 12–13).

This prayer, with its poetry about God's victory over death, is used during the Jewish holiday Chanukah (meaning "rededication") every winter. In addition, the psalm is so beautiful and victorious in its tone and content that Jews have come to use it as a dedication for the house of worship, where we gather as a community, and our family home, the true house of God.

In Jewish tradition, the family home is more important than the synagogue. It is in our homes that our children receive their first education in faith and where families experience the illnesses, sorrows, and joys of life. And the home is where the *Shechinah*, the presence of God, dwells in our midst. For this reason, Psalm 30 is read at new home dedications.

"But as for me and my household, we will serve the LORD" (Joshua 24:15, NIV).

PRAYER

1. Read Psalm 30.

2. Recite the following blessing in Hebrew or English:

Baruch Ata A-do-nai Elo-heinu Melech Haolam she-hech-e-ya-nu v'ki-ma-nu v'hi-gi-ya-nu li-z'man hazeh.

Praised are You, Lord our God, King of the Universe, who has granted us life, sustained us, and enabled us to reach this occasion.

Courage for the Real World

For the Leader. A Psalm of David.

In thee, O LORD, have I taken refuge;
    let me never be ashamed;
    Deliver me in Thy righteousness.
Incline Thine ear unto me, deliver me speedily;
    Be Thou to me a rock of refuge, even a
        fortress of defence, to save me.
For Thou art my rock and my fortress;
    Therefore for Thy name's sake lead me and guide me.
Bring me forth out of the net that they
        have hidden for me;
    For Thou art my stronghold.
Into Thy hand I commit my spirit;
    Thou hast redeemed me, O LORD, Thou God of truth.
I hate them that regard lying vanities;
    But I trust in the LORD.

I will be glad and rejoice in Thy lovingkindness;
For Thou hast seen mine affliction,
Thou hast taken cognizance of the
troubles of my soul,
And Thou hast not given me over into
the hand of the enemy;
Thou hast set my feet in a broad place.

Be gracious unto me, O LORD, for I am in distress;
Mine eye wasteth away with vexation,
yea, my soul and my body.
For my life is spent in sorrow, and my years in sighing;
My strength faileth because of mine iniquity,
and my bones are wasted away. . . .

O love the LORD, all ye His godly ones;
The LORD preserveth the faithful,
And plentifully repayeth him that acteth haughtily.
Be strong, and let your heart take courage,
All ye that wait for the LORD.
(Psalm 31:1–11, 24–25)

Many people believe that in a perfect world, good prospers and evil is punished. But as the Bible often shows, we do not live in a perfect world. Corruption is rampant. Wars and atrocities are reported daily on the news.

Economies collapse. Natural disasters destroy homes. It can be difficult to make sense of the world. We wonder whether God is really good. And if he is, why does he allow good people to suffer? Perhaps he is not able to overcome the bad.

However, various Bible writers point out that God is aware of our suffering. For example, Job 36:15 states, "But those who suffer he delivers in their suffering; he speaks to them in their affliction" (NIV). And, as David prays in Psalm 31, when we commit ourselves to God, salvation comes: "Into Thy hand I commit my spirit; Thou hast redeemed me, O Lord, Thou God of truth" (verse 6).

In Psalm 31, David, even as a king, does not describe life as a utopia without hardship. He is transparent in this prayer about the suffering he endures. But David boldly claims that God helps him through pain and suffering for God's purposes. Apparently he believes God is not only good but also able to overcome the bad.

David describes threats against his physical, emotional, and spiritual life. First, in verse 7, David asks for protection from those who "regard lying vanities." During this time, the nations surrounding Israel, and even some Israelites, are practicing idol worship. Psalm 106:36 says: "They served their idols, which became a snare unto them."

Then, in verse 12, David describes "adversaries" who cause David's neighbors and friends to disdain him. These enemies gossip about him and even plot to kill him (verse 14). We can imagine that these death threats caused him to struggle with fear and anxiety.

All this has taken a tremendous emotional toll on David, who expresses his spiritual and emotional "affliction" and "troubles of [his] soul" (verse 8). He adds that his "eye wasteth away with vexation"; he is physically wasting away (verse 10).

In several remarkable and profound statements, David explains that struggle, grief, fear, and sorrow—real-world suffering—have not prevented God from redeeming him (verse 6). He adds that harrowing problems have not stopped him from experiencing God's "abundant" goodness in the face of adversity (verse 20) or God's faithfulness in periods of severe suffering (verse 22).

We can comprehend why David would seek God's help and protection in this often cruel world. In verses 3–4, David calls upon God to be his rock and to protect him as if he were in a fortress. As we consider our own responses to turbulent, frightening situations, we can gain insights from David's approach to finding meaning and protection in a broken world. He says: "O love the LORD, all ye His godly ones; the LORD preserveth the faithful, and plentifully repayeth him that acteth haughtily. Be strong, and let your heart take courage, all ye that wait for the LORD" (verses 24–25).

David's psalm might also inspire us to live with strength and courage in a severely broken world. For David, the source of this courage was God, not himself: "But as for me, I have trusted in Thee, O LORD; I have said: 'Thou art my God' " (verse 15).

PRAYER

We give thanks to you because you are our Lord our God and the God of our fathers for ever and ever; you are the Rock of our lives, the Shield of our salvation through every generation. We will give thanks to you and declare your praise for our lives that are committed into your hand, and for our souls that are in your charge, and for your miracles that are daily with us, and for your wonders and benefits that you provide at all times, evening, morning, and noon. O you who are always good, whose mercies fail not; whose loving-kindnesses never cease, we have ever hoped in you.

Whom to Follow?

*For the Leader. [A Psalm] of David the servant
of the LORD.*

*Transgression speaketh to the wicked, methinks—
    There is no fear of God before his eyes.
For it flattereth him in his eyes,
    Until his iniquity be found, and he be hated.
The words of his mouth are iniquity and deceit;
    He hath left off to be wise, to do good.
He deviseth iniquity upon his bed;
    He setteth himself in a way that is not good;
    He abhorreth not evil.*

*Thy lovingkindness, O LORD, is in the heavens;
    Thy faithfulness reacheth unto the skies.
Thy righteousness is like the mighty mountains;
    Thy judgments are like the great deep;
    Man and beast Thou preservest, O LORD.
How precious is Thy lovingkindness, O God!*

And the children of men take refuge
in the shadow of Thy wings.
They are abundantly satisfied with
the fatness of Thy house;
And Thou makest them drink of the
river of Thy pleasures.
For with Thee is the fountain of life;
In Thy light do we see light.

O continue Thy lovingkindness unto
them that know Thee;
And Thy righteousness to the upright in heart.
Let not the foot of pride overtake me,
And let not the hand of the wicked drive me away.
There are the workers of iniquity fallen;
They are thrust down, and are not
able to rise. (Psalm 36)

David, like great poets, uses literary devices to make his prayers come alive. One of those is personification, which gives human characteristics to feelings or ideas.

In this psalm, David personifies transgression: "Transgression speaketh to the wicked, methinks—there is no fear of God before his eyes. For it flattereth him in his eyes, until his iniquity be found, and he be hated" (verses 2–3).

David says that a wicked person has no fear of God. Many Bible scholars teach that without a fear of God, people can often be led to believe they can do whatever they want without negative consequences. At night in bed, covered by darkness, the wicked person plots and plans against God and others (verse 5). So, as those who follow transgression fall further into sin, they abandon doing what is good (verse 4) and are eventually "thrust down . . . not able to rise" (verse 13).

As we read about the delusion and consequences of transgression, we may wonder why anyone would follow it. This is even harder to understand when we read, in verses 6–11, what David writes about the benefits of following God. David says that God cares deeply about humanity and all creation. In contrast to the destructive path of transgression, David reminds us that we can experience the protection of God's "wings" (*kenafav*) and drink from his "fountain of life" (the Torah, according to Jewish tradition) that nourishes our souls.

Transgression tempts us in the darkness of night, but God gives us his light to spread through deeds of compassion, mercy, and truth (verses 10–11). According to this psalm, the outcomes of these two distinct directions—transgression or righteousness—are literally like the difference between night and day. One leads to angst and death; the other leads to beauty and peace.

David prays at the end of this psalm for the welfare of those who know him—that God may grant them blessings and care. Then David asks God to save him from the "foot of pride" and the "hand of the wicked" (verse 12). In these final requests, he states that he does not want to end up where "the workers of iniquity" lie "fallen" (verse 13).

This psalm also has a strong connection to the book of Proverbs, believed by many to be primarily written by David's son Solomon. In Proverbs 9, we see the personification of both folly (transgression) and wisdom (light). David and Solomon both come to the same conclusion: without the fear of God, transgression and folly can control our lives.

In David's prayer in Psalm 36, we read that the wicked person has "no fear of God before his eyes" (verse 2), while Proverbs 9:10–12 states, "The fear of the LORD is the beginning of wisdom, and knowledge of the Holy One is understanding. For through wisdom your days will be many, and years will be added to your life. If you are wise, your wisdom will reward you; if you are a mocker, you alone will suffer" (NIV).

In Jewish tradition, blessings and curses (good and evil) are personified as the *Yetzer Ha-Tov*, the good inclination, and the *Yetzer Ha-Ra*, the evil inclination. The latter speaks to us through rationalization and pride, convincing us that we deserve to indulge ourselves in seduction.

The former calls us to be strong, to pray, and to turn aside from temptation. The rabbis of the first century understood this when they wrote, "Who is strong? He who conquers his evil inclination, and one who rules over his spirit" (*Ethics of the Fathers*, chapter 4). Both the *Yetzer Ha-Ra* and the *Yetzer Ha-Tov* speak to us daily through the still, small voice of conscience, calling us to do *mitzvot* (deeds of righteousness) or *averot* (deeds of evil and sin).

As David writes in his prayer, temptation offers us choices that may seem easy but lead us away from God and his commandments. Prayer, good deeds, and the fear of God—according to the psalm—lead us in the right direction, helping us to see and be God's light in the darkness. May we pray as David prayed: "For with Thee is the fountain of life; in Thy light do we see light" (verse 10).

PRAYER

Cause us, O Lord our God, to lie down in peace, and raise us up, O our King, unto life. Spread over us the tabernacle of your peace. Direct us rightly through your own good counsel. Save us for your name's sake. Be a shield about us; remove from us every enemy, pestilence, sword, famine, and sorrow; remove also the adversary from before us and from behind us. O shelter us beneath the shadow of your wings, for you, O God, are our guardian and deliverer. Yes, you, O God, are a gracious and merciful King. Guard our going out and coming in unto life and unto peace from this time forth and for evermore. Blessed are you, O Lord, who guards your people Israel forever.

Forgiveness That Leads to Peace

A Psalm of David, to make memorial.

O LORD, rebuke me not in Thine anger;
Neither chasten me in Thy wrath.
For Thine arrows are gone deep into me,
And Thy hand is come down upon me.
There is no soundness in my flesh because
of Thine indignation;
Neither is there any health in my bones because of my sin.
For mine iniquities are gone over my head;
As a heavy burden they are too heavy for me.
My wounds are noisome, they fester,
Because of my foolishness.
I am bent and bowed down greatly;
I go mourning all the day.
For my loins are filled with burning;
And there is no soundness in my flesh.

I am benumbed and sore crushed;
I groan by reason of the moaning of my heart.
Lord, all my desire is before Thee;
And my sighing is not hid from Thee. . . .

. . .

For I do declare mine iniquity;
I am full of care because of my sin.
But mine enemies are strong in health;
And they that hate me wrongfully are multiplied.
They also that repay evil for good
Are adversaries unto me, because I
follow the thing that is good.
Forsake me not, O LORD;
O my God, be not far from me.
Make haste to help me,
O Lord, my salvation. (Psalm 38:1–10, 19–23)

This psalm portrays David as sick, abandoned, and persecuted because of his sins. Overwhelmed by the weight of his guilt, David confesses, "For mine iniquities are gone over my head; as a heavy burden they are too heavy for me" (verse 5). Jewish tradition teaches that this prayer serves as a reminder of not only David's suffering but also the suffering of the people of Israel.

As the prayer opens, David begs God not to punish him further. He has already suffered from God's anger, and he can take no more (verses 3–4). In verses 4–9, David describes how his guilt is affecting his body. He says, "There is no . . . health in my bones because of my sin" (verse 4). His "wounds are noisome, they fester" (verse 6); he is bent over in severe depression. In a psychosomatic state, he is sick, feverish, and weak as a result of the "moaning of [his] heart" (verse 9).

Unable to withstand all the burdens of his guilt—the pain, depression, and sorrow—David calls out to God, who already knows about David's innermost anguish (verse 10). He longs for deliverance and begs God not to abandon him (verses 22–23).

Peace, in Hebrew, is *shalom*, which comes from the root *shalaym*, meaning "wholeness." In this psalm David expresses what is happening to him as a result of straying from God: he loses that sense of wholeness and peace. His wrongdoing fractures his inner being, causing the turmoil described in the words of his prayer. In his state of unrepentance, David does not experience inner peace (wholeness); but when he repents, "I do declare mine iniquity" (verse 19), he throws himself into the care of God (verses 22–23) to reestablish wholeness with God and with his own conscience.

As we read this transparent prayer of David, we can see how difficult life can become if we don't acknowledge our wrongdoing. But we also see how powerful confession can be in leading us to *shleymut*—wholeness in our souls and in our relationships with God and others.

PRAYER

May it then be your will, O Lord our God and God of our fathers, to forgive us for all our sins, to pardon us for all our iniquities, and to grant us remission for all our transgressions.

For the sin that we have committed before you under compulsion, or of our own will;

And for the sin that we have committed before you in hardening of the heart;

For the sin that we have committed before you unknowingly;

And for the sin that we have committed before you openly and secretly;

For the sin that we have committed before you knowingly and deceitfully;

And for the sin that we have committed before you by the sinful meditating of the heart;

And for the sin that we have committed before you wittingly or unwittingly;

For all these, O God of forgiveness, forgive us, pardon us, grant us remission.

Forgive us, O our Father, for we have sinned; pardon us, O our King, for we have transgressed;

For you pardon and forgive. Blessed are you, O Lord. You are gracious and abundantly forgive. Amen.

What Does It All Mean?

For the Leader for Jeduthun. A psalm of David.

I said: "I will take heed to my ways,
That I sin not with my tongue;
I will keep a curb upon my mouth,
While the wicked is before me."
I was dumb with silence; I held my peace, had no comfort;
And my pain was held in check.
My heart waxed hot within me;
While I was musing, the fire kindled;
Then spoke I with my tongue:

"LORD, make me to know mine end,
And the measure of my days, what it is;
Let me know how short-lived I am.
Behold, Thou hast made my days as hand-breadths;
And mine age is as nothing before Thee;

Surely every man at his best estate
is altogether vanity.

Selah

Surely man walketh as a mere semblance;
Surely for vanity they are in turmoil;
He heapeth up riches, and knoweth
not who shall gather them.
And now, Lord, what wait I for?
My hope, it is in Thee.
Deliver me from all my transgressions;
Make me not the reproach of the base.
I am dumb, I open not my mouth;
Because Thou hast done it.
Remove Thy stroke from off me;
I am consumed by the blow of Thy hand.
With rebukes dost Thou chasten man for iniquity,
And like a moth Thou makest
his beauty to consume away;
Surely every man is vanity.

Selah

Hear my prayer, O LORD, and give ear unto my cry;
Keep not silence at my tears;
For I am a stranger with Thee,
A sojourner, as all my fathers were.
Look away from me, that I may take comfort,
Before I go hence, and be no more." (Psalm 39)

If given the opportunity to stand on a high mountain far from a city, a person could take in a spectacular view of the vast universe—and perhaps observe meteors burning and vanishing from the backdrop of the Milky Way. Looking up at the billions of stars could make any of us feel very small and wonder what, if any, significance life has.

David experiences this, as described in Psalm 8. "When I look at your heavens, the work of your fingers, the moon and the stars, which you have set in place, what is man that you are mindful of him, and the son of man that you care for him?" (verses 3–4, ESV).

In Psalm 39, David struggles again with the same question. He is going through a time of emotional distress (verses 3–4). David finally speaks out, asking God the questions that have been burning in his heart (verse 4). His words echo what he wrote in Psalm 8. In this prayer David cries out, "LORD, make me to know mine end, and the measure of my days" (verse 5). He tells God, "Behold, Thou hast made my days as hand-breadths" (verse 6) and "Surely man walketh as a mere semblance" (verse 7). He adds that accumulating wealth is tenuous (verse 7).

In verse 8, David summarizes his profound observations with a question: "And now, Lord, what wait I for?" It is a question many people ask at one time or another. Human beings seem to have a deep need to know what our lives mean.

David's answer immediately follows his question. In the same verse, David responds by identifying God as his only source of hope. "My hope, it is in Thee," he says.

If God is his hope, David appears to express his desire to not let anything come between him and God. Perhaps for this reason, in verse 9, he asks God to save him from his transgressions. He acknowledges his mortality and the brevity of his life, but he pleads with God to end his punishment and to hear his cry (verses 11–13).

Reading this prayer, we can ask the same questions David asked. What is the meaning of our short lives? Do we simply hustle and bustle through life, accumulating wealth or power? Or, as David asks, is there more to it?

In this psalm, David's conclusion is that God gives his life meaning. In other psalms, a similar viewpoint is conveyed. In Psalm 119:147, the psalmist defines his hope this way: "I rise before dawn and cry for help; I have put my hope in your word" (NIV). In the Jewish tradition, the meaning of life is in the Torah, which is held up as God's eternal message to each generation.

As David grapples with his seeming insignificance in relation to the heavens, he believes that despite his short life span, God thinks of him and gives him meaning. "You have made [humankind] a little lower than the heavenly beings and crowned him with glory and honor" (Psalm 8:5, ESV).

PRAYER

Lord, what is man, that you regard him? Or the son of man, that you take account of him? Man is like to vanity; his days are as a shadow that passes away. In the morning he flourishes, and sprouts afresh; in the evening he is cut down, and withers. So teach us to number our days, that we may get us a heart of wisdom. Mark the innocent person, and behold the upright: for the latter end of that person is peace. But God will redeem my soul from the grasp of the grave: for he will receive me. My flesh and my heart fail, but God is the strength of my heart and my portion forever. And the dust returns to the earth as it was, but the spirit returns to God, who gave it. I shall behold your face in righteousness; I shall be satisfied, when I awake, with your likeness. Amen.

23

Keeping the King Humble

For the Leader. A Psalm of David.

I waited patiently for the LORD;
And He inclined unto me, and heard my cry.
He brought me up also out of the tumultuous
pit, out of the miry clay;
And He set my feet upon a rock,
He established my goings.
And He hath put a new song in my mouth, even
praise unto our God; Many shall see, and fear,
And shall trust in the LORD.

Happy is the man that hath made the LORD his trust,
And hath not turned unto the arrogant, nor
unto such as fall away treacherously.
Many things hast Thou done, O LORD my God,

Even Thy wonderful works,
*   and Thy thoughts toward us;*
There is none to be compared unto Thee!
If I would declare and speak of them,
They are more than can be told.
Sacrifice and meal-offering Thou hast no delight in;
*   Mine ears hast Thou opened;*
*   Burnt-offering and sin-offering hast Thou not required.*
Then said I: "Lo, I am come
*   With the roll of a book which is prescribed for me;*
I delight to do Thy will, O my God;
*   Yea, Thy law is in my inmost parts."*
I have preached righteousness in the great congregation,
*   Lo, I did not refrain my lips;*
*   O Lord, Thou knowest.*
I have not hid Thy righteousness within my heart;
*   I have declared Thy faithfulness and Thy salvation;*
*   I have not concealed Thy mercy and Thy*
*   truth from the great congregation.*
Thou, O Lord, wilt not withhold Thy
*   compassions from me;*
*   Let Thy mercy and Thy truth*
*   continually preserve me. . . .*

But, as for me, that am poor and needy,
*   The Lord will account it unto me;*
*   Thou art my help and my deliverer;*
*   O my God, tarry not. (Psalm 40:1–12, 18)*

As shown in Deuteronomy 17:18–20, God commanded the kings of Israel to have a copy of God's laws with them on the throne and to observe the law faithfully. God wants the kings to be well versed in his laws in order to lead the nation well.

Moreover, this command is given so that the king "may learn to fear the LORD his God by keeping all the words of this law . . . that his heart may not be lifted up above his brothers" (Deuteronomy 17:19–20, ESV). This passage in the Bible makes it clear that humility is essential to good leadership.

As king, David is commanded in Deuteronomy 17:18 to write a copy of the first five books of the Bible (the Torah) in a book. He is not allowed to have a scribe or servant do it; he must complete the scroll himself. By writing each word of the text, David learns more about God and his commandments.

And so, in Psalm 40 David says, "I delight to do Thy will, O my God; yea, Thy law is in my inmost parts" (verse 9). His deep understanding of God's laws and principles for life leads David to sing "a new song" (verse 4) about the happiness of those who trust in God rather than in arrogant and evil people (verse 5). David believes God is trustworthy because God has multiplied his "wonderful works" and his "thoughts toward" humankind (verse 6).

As king, David mentions the scroll of God's law (verses 8–9), which refers to the law God gave to the people at Mount Sinai. Importantly, David desires for God's covenant to remain in his heart, in his "inmost parts" (verse 9), not just on the scroll. This statement by David is similar to what Jeremiah wrote many years later: "I will put my law in their minds and write it on their hearts. I will be their God, and they will be my people" (Jeremiah 31:33, NIV).

Although David appears to have made a full effort to internalize God's law, in this prayer he also says he is making every effort to proclaim God's "righteousness in the great congregation" (verse 10). He also speaks of God's deliverance, faithfulness, salvation, mercy, and compassion (verses 11–12). In this prayer, we can see the inward impact of God's laws in David's life and his desire to share them with others.

Based on the last verse of Psalm 40, it appears that David is echoing the command in Deuteronomy 17 for kings to be humble before God. He says, "But, as for me, that am poor and needy, the Lord will account it unto me." And in this humility, David finds that God is his help and deliverer (verse 18).

Whether one is Jewish or not, reading the Bible can be a daily practice. Perhaps by doing so, by writing God's words on our hearts, we can remain humble before others and make wise decisions.

PRAYER

Baruch Atah Adonai, Blessed are you, O Lord our God, King of the universe, who has sanctified us by your commandments, and commanded us to occupy ourselves with the words of the Law.

Make pleasant, therefore, we ask you, O Lord our God, the words of your Law in our mouth and in the mouth of your people, the house of Israel, so that we with our offspring and the offspring of your people, the house of Israel, may all know your name and learn your Law. Blessed are you, O Lord, who teaches the Law to your people Israel.

Baruch Atah Adonai, Blessed are you, O Lord our God, King of the universe, who has chosen us from all nations and given us your Law. Blessed are you, O Lord, who gives the Law.

24

A Pure Heart

For the Leader. A Psalm of David; when Nathan the prophet came unto him, after he had gone in to Bath-sheba.

Be gracious unto me, O God,
according to Thy mercy;
According to the multitude of Thy compassions
blot out my transgressions.
Wash me thoroughly from mine iniquity,
And cleanse me from my sin.
For I know my transgressions;
And my sin is ever before me.
Against Thee, Thee only, have I sinned,
And done that which is evil in Thy sight;
That Thou mayest be justified when Thou speakest,
And be in the right when Thou judgest.

Behold, I was brought forth in iniquity,
And in sin did my mother conceive me.
Behold, Thou desirest truth in the inward parts;

Make me, therefore, to know wisdom
*   in mine inmost heart.*
Purge me with hyssop, and I shall be clean;
*   Wash me, and I shall be whiter than snow.*
Make me to hear joy and gladness;
*   That the bones which Thou hast crushed may rejoice.*
Hide Thy face from my sins,
*   And blot out all mine iniquities.*
Create me a clean heart, O God;
*   And renew a stedfast spirit within me. . . .*

. . .

For Thou delightest not in sacrifice, else would I give it;
*   Thou hast no pleasure in burnt-offering.*
The sacrifices of God are a broken spirit;
*   A broken and a contrite heart, O God, Thou*
*   wilt not despise. (Psalm 51:1–12, 18–19)*

I n this prayer, David pleads for God to restore his soul after a terrible series of wrongdoings. The psalm is David's confession after his adultery with Bathsheba and his decision to send her husband to the front lines of battle. The full story can be found in 2 Samuel 11–12.

At first, David attempts to hide what he has done. When he finds out Bathsheba is pregnant with his child, he makes sure her husband dies in battle and then marries Bathsheba, who eventually gives birth to a son. But the prophet Nathan confronts David regarding the adultery with a story about a rich man with many sheep who stole the one ewe lamb that his neighbor owned. David realizes he has been found out and immediately admits that he has sinned before God.

David's prompt acknowledgment of his sin saves his family line, but the outcomes of his decisions are still severe. The first child he conceived with Bathsheba perishes. David's anguish through this tragedy is conveyed in 2 Samuel 12:16: "David pleaded with God for the child. He fasted and spent the nights lying in sackcloth on the ground" (NIV). Later, David's son Absalom rebels against him (2 Samuel 15).

At the writing of Psalm 51, David is alone and disgraced. His sin is great, and the consequences are insupportable. In addition, he knows he has failed God. He says to God, "Against Thee, Thee only, have I sinned, and done that which is evil in Thy sight" (verse 6). David seeks to repair that relationship. He pours out his heart to God, who is faithful and compassionate (verse 3), and asks God to "wash" him (verses 4 and 9).

Even in this difficult moment, David acknowledges his sin without making excuses for his behavior (verses 5–6). His honesty differentiates him from Saul, who failed to heed God's command and then made excuses for his sin (1 Samuel 15). David respects God's justice and is willing to accept the consequences of his actions. David knows he is capable of doing evil, saying, "Behold, I was brought forth in iniquity, and in sin did my mother conceive me" (verse 7), and he relies on God's cleansing forgiveness (verse 9).

One remarkable insight from David is his recognition that restoration will require something far deeper than just religious rituals such as sacrifices and burnt offerings (verse 18). He concludes that the first step to true restoration is a "broken and a contrite heart" (verse 19), a heart full of true sorrow that mourns separation from God. This profound state of humility and surrender can be understood in David's experience as the doorway to forgiveness and healing.

David's prayer can be seen as a process for responding to wrongdoing. The outcome hinges on David's honest admission of what he's done. He assumes responsibility. He confesses that he has broken God's commandments, hurt other people, and ruptured his relationship with God. His confession is not skin deep. He expresses his anguish and sincerely laments what he has done. His sorrow is deep and real.

This psalm never indicates whether David experiences the shalom, or wholeness, he prays for. But God remains faithful to his promise to sustain David's lineage. Perhaps the sign of God's forgiveness is that Solomon, David's second son with Bathsheba, is chosen to ascend the throne after David, with the support of Nathan the prophet (1 Kings 1).

We cannot fully know the extent to which David carried the burden of his sin with him through his life. But many passages throughout the Bible indicate that God restores and redeems people when they call to him. "I have swept away your offenses like a cloud, your sins like the morning mist. Return to me, for I have redeemed you" (Isaiah 44:22, NIV).

PRAYER

A song of ascents.

Out of the depths I cry to you, LORD;
 LORD, hear my voice.
Let your ears be attentive
 to my cry for mercy.

If you, LORD, kept a record of sins,
 LORD, who could stand?
But with you there is forgiveness,
 so that we can, with reverence, serve you.

I wait for the LORD, my whole being waits,
 and in his word I put my hope.
I wait for the LORD
 more than watchmen wait for the morning,
 more than watchmen wait for the morning.

Israel, put your hope in the LORD,
 for with the LORD is unfailing love
 and with him is full redemption.
He himself will redeem Israel
 from all their sins. (Psalm 130, NIV)

Lean on God

For the Leader; with string-music. Maschil of David:
when the Ziphites came and said to Saul:
"Doth not David hide himself with us?"

O God, save me by Thy name,
    And right me by Thy might.
O God, hear my prayer; give ear to
        the words of my mouth.
For strangers are risen up against me,
    And violent men have sought after my soul;
    They have not set God before them.

                            Selah

Behold, God is my helper;
    The Lord is for me as the upholder of my soul.
He will requite the evil unto them
        that lie in wait for me;
    Destroy Thou them in Thy truth.
With a freewill-offering will I sacrifice unto Thee;

I will give thanks unto Thy name,
   O Lord, for it is good.
For He hath delivered me out of all trouble;
   And mine eye hath gazed upon
      mine enemies. (Psalm 54)

Perhaps one of the most painful things in life occurs when a close friend or relative turns against us. The trust on which the relationship was built crumbles, which makes reconciliation hard to imagine. As the well-known artist Walter Anderson (1903–1965) said, "Trust is like a vase . . . once it's broken, though you can fix it, the vase will never be same again."

A terrible betrayal provides the context for David's prayer in Psalm 54. The moment that Samuel anoints David as the new king, the *Shekinah* (God's Spirit or presence) leaves the rejected King Saul and rests on David (1 Samuel 16:13–14). Saul becomes a tormented man. He brings David to his court to soothe his emotional turmoil through music but realizes that David now has God's Spirit (1 Samuel 18:12); therefore, he attempts to kill David (1 Samuel 19:9–23).

David escapes into the Judean wilderness, his own tribal land, to elude Saul. Several miles southeast of Hebron in the hill country of Judah lies the city of Ziph. This wilderness area provides a hiding place for David and his men as King Saul pursues them. However, the Ziphites also betray David by pointing out his hideout to the king. Now Saul, whom David loved, and the Ziphites have turned on him. David is warned and manages to escape Saul's threat (1 Samuel 23:14–29).

In Psalm 54, David asks God for protection and vindication (verse 3). He has done nothing wrong, yet he has been betrayed and pursued. He asks God to hear his prayer (verse 4), telling God that "strangers" and "violent men"—Saul and his army—seek his death (verse 5).

Reading the psalm, we can imagine that David is afraid, hurt, angry, and tired. And so he looks for God's help and support. He pleads with God for justice, to see the destruction of his betrayers and his pursuers, because God is faithful (verse 7). David believes that God's hand will save him and help him triumph over his foes (verse 9).

Many people feel betrayed at one time or another. And it's possible that we have betrayed someone else—perhaps we've gossiped with malicious intent, broken a marriage vow, or failed to fulfill a business contract. Versions of the betrayals David experienced play out in our lives also. When we forsake God by betraying each other, it leaves a stain on our souls. Isaac Bashevis Singer, a famous Jewish author, said: "When you betray somebody else, you also betray yourself."

David's prayer in Psalm 54 also helps us reflect on how we might respond when someone betrays us. David decides he will lean on God, who is faithful. "Behold, God is my helper; the Lord is for me as the upholder of my soul" (verse 6).

PRAYER

True and firm, established and enduring, right and faithful, beloved and precious, desirable and pleasant, revered and mighty, well-ordered and acceptable, good and beautiful is this your word unto us for ever and ever. It is true, the God of the universe is our King, the Rock of Jacob, the Shield of our salvation: throughout all generations he endures and his name endures; his throne is established, and his kingdom and his faithfulness endure forever. His words also live and endure; they are faithful and desirable for ever and to all eternity, as for our fathers so also for us, our children, our generations, and for all the generations of the seed of Israel his servants.

For the first and for the last ages your word is good and endures for ever and ever; it is true and trustworthy, a statute that shall not pass away. True it is that you are indeed the Lord our God, and the God of our fathers, our King, our fathers' King, our Redeemer, the Redeemer of our fathers, our Maker, the Rock of our salvation; our Deliverer and Rescuer from everlasting, such is your name; there is no God beside you.

Protecting Friendship

For the Leader; with string-music. Maschil of David.

Give ear, O God, to my prayer;
  And hide not Thyself from my supplication.
Attend unto me, and answer me;
  I am distraught in my complaint, and will moan;
Because of the voice of the enemy,
  Because of the oppression of the wicked;
  For they cast mischief upon me,
  And in anger they persecute me.
My heart doth writhe within me;
  And the terrors of death are fallen upon me.
Fear and trembling come upon me, And
    horror hath overwhelmed me.
And I said: "Oh that I had wings like a dove!
  Then would I fly away, and be at rest.
Lo, then would I wander far off,
  I would lodge in the wilderness.

                                        Selah

I would haste me to a shelter
  From the stormy wind and tempest."
Destroy, O Lord, and divide their tongue;
  For I have seen violence and strife in the city.
Day and night they go about it upon the walls thereof;
  Iniquity also and mischief are in the midst of it.
Wickedness is in the midst thereof;
  Oppression and guile depart not from her broad place.
For it was not an enemy that taunted me,
  Then I could have borne it;
  Neither was it mine adversary that did
    magnify himself against me,
  Then I would have hid myself from him.
But it was thou, a man mine equal,
  My companion, and my familiar friend;
We took sweet counsel together,
  In the house of God we walked with the throng.
May He incite death against them,
  Let them go down alive into the nether-world;
  For evil is in their dwelling, and within them.
As for me, I will call upon God;
  And the LORD shall save me.
Evening, and morning, and at noon,
    will I complain, and moan;
  And He hath heard my voice.
He hath redeemed my soul in peace so
    that none came nigh me;
  For they were many that strove with me.

God shall hear, and humble them,
  Even He that is enthroned of old,

                                                              Selah

  Such as have no changes,
    And fear not God.
  He hath put forth his hands against them
      that were at peace with him;
    He hath profaned his covenant.
  Smoother than cream were the speeches of his mouth,
    But his heart was war;
    His words were softer than oil,
    Yet were they keen-edged swords. (Psalm 55:1–22)

According to Jewish tradition, David wrote this psalm as a response to the rebellion of his son Absalom. This betrayal leaves David brokenhearted, as described in 2 Samuel 15:30: "But David continued up the Mount of Olives, weeping as he went; his head was covered and he was barefoot. All the people with him covered their heads too and were weeping as they went up" (NIV). Moreover, Ahithophel, one of David's best friends, counselors, and companions, defects to support Absalom (2 Samuel 15:31, 16:21).

It's possible that David wrote Psalm 55 about a different conflict. Some event or series of conflicts has resulted in difficulties that are almost more than David can bear.

His sadness and anger fill this prayer; he mourns with dirge-like language: "My heart doth writhe within me; and the terrors of death are fallen upon me" (verse 5).

In the first part of the prayer, David calls upon God to intervene. Perhaps this is his plea for help against Absalom's rebellion. He is harassed, oppressed, and filled with dread (verses 4–5). David is also afraid (verse 6). This fear could be related to his flight from his palace to save his life and the lives of his family members when Absalom's rebellion is temporarily successful (2 Samuel 15:14). David knows that Absalom has already murdered his half brother, Amnon (2 Samuel 13:23–39), and David probably feels that Absalom will kill him too.

David wants to escape this fearful situation. He cries, "Oh that I had wings like a dove! Then I would fly away, and be at rest . . . in the wilderness" (verses 7–8). He longs to flee to a place away from the chaos and corruption that reigns in the city (verses 9–12).

In verses 13–14, David turns his focus to the defection of his friend. He says he can bear an enemy who denounces and disparages him, but the betrayal of his friend and counselor breaks his heart. David is probably referring to Ahithophel, who was his mentor, not a servant (verse 14). Together they walked as friends and confidantes (verse 15).

David's anger becomes evident when he asks God to curse the defector. He asks God to send the person to "the nether-world" (*Sheol*, the grave) alive, possibly so that he will suffer the way David is suffering (verse 16).

After venting his anger, David manages his emotions by turning to God, saying, "As for me, I will call upon God; and the LORD shall save me" (verse 17). David states that God hears his voice and redeems him unharmed from the battle waging against him (verses 18–20).

The sad underlying story of this prayer is David's lost friendship. Considering this psalm, we can see that our friendships can be fragile; therefore, they need to be nurtured and protected. We need to keep our friends close by, listening to them, respecting their choices, and being faithful through good times and bad. As Samuel Johnson, the well-known poet and writer said, "A man should keep his friendship in constant repair."

"For my brothers and companions' sake I will say, 'Peace be within you!'" (Psalm 122:8, ESV).

PRAYER

Adonai, Lord, you are a friend to the friendless. Help me to be a good friend, to listen without judgment, to act only in faith, and to keep my commitments. May you bless all my friends and family with the gift of your shalom, and grant us the wisdom to never take our relationship with you for granted. Amen!

27

Transcending Fear

*For the Leader; upon Jonath-elem-rehokim. [A Psalm]
of David; Michtam; when the Philistines took him in Gath.*

> *Be gracious unto me, O God, for man
>   would swallow me up;
>   All the day he fighting oppresseth me.
> They that lie in wait for me would
>   swallow me up all the day;
>   For they are many that fight against
>   me, O Most High,
> In the day that I am afraid,
>   I will put my trust in Thee.
> In God—I will praise His word—
>   In God do I trust, I will not be afraid;
>   What can flesh do unto me?*
>
> *All the day they trouble mine affairs;
>   All their thoughts are against me for evil.
> They gather themselves together, they hide themselves,*

They mark my steps;
According as they have waited for my soul.
Because of iniquity cast them out;
In anger bring down the peoples, O God.
Thou has counted my wanderings;
Put Thou my tears into Thy bottle;
Are they not in Thy book?
Then shall mine enemies turn back
in the day that I call;
This I know, that God is for me.
In God—I will praise His word—
In the LORD—I will praise His word—
In God do I trust, I will not be afraid;
What can man do unto me? (Psalm 56:1–12)

The backstory of this prayer occurs when David, in order to seek refuge from Saul, decides to hide among the Philistines in Gath (1 Samuel 21:10). When David is recognized as the one who had killed "tens of thousands" of Philistines, he fears for his life and escapes death by pretending to be insane (1 Samuel 21:11–15). David and his men later return to Gath and serve Achish, the king of Gath, in battles against his enemies (1 Samuel 27).

In his prayer in Psalm 56, David is struggling with fear (verse 4). The mighty warrior, slayer of Goliath, and soon to be king is in enemy territory, and Saul wants him dead. During this time in David's life, there is no rest for him. There is nowhere to go—except to God.

In Psalm 56:4–5, David looks his fear in the face and calls on God. David not only trusts God when he needs help but also praises God (verse 11), even in a time of death threats. He shows that his devotion to God is not limited to fair weather and beds of roses. This attitude and practice seem to help David overcome his fear. He recognizes that with God, no human being can harm him (verses 5 and 12).

It's most likely that verses 6–8 of the psalm address not the Philistines but the Israelites who have driven David to seek shelter in enemy territory. They undermine his cause, stir up strife, and plot against him (1 Samuel 19–25). David prays for God to punish them and "cast them out" because of their "iniquity" (verse 8).

David has no doubt that God has kept a record of his trials and tears, so many tears that they could fill a bottle (verse 9). Despite the threats against his life, David knows with all his heart that God is with him and for him (verses 10–12). Believing this, David repeats the heart of his prayer: "In God do I trust, I will not be afraid; what can man do unto me?" (verse 12).

Most of us will never face the types of death threats, imprisonments, and betrayal that David experienced. But we do live in stressful times. Many fear unemployment, health problems, relational tensions, and a long list of other concerns. This prayer provides us with an opportunity to consider the ways we can live courageously through our fears. And as for David, he took his fears to God while in the presence of his enemies.

PRAYER

Each prayer begins with the phrase *Baruch Atah Adonai, Eloheinu Melech HaOlam* ("Blessed are you, O Lord our God, King of the universe")

Blessed are you, O Lord our God, King of the universe, who . . .

has given to the rooster intelligence to distinguish between day and night.

has not made me a slave.

opens the eyes of the blind.

clothes the naked.

frees those who are bound.

raises up those who are bowed down.

spreads forth the earth above the waters.

has supplied my every want.

has made firm the steps of humankind.

girds Israel with might.

crowns Israel with glory.

gives strength to the weary.

A Personal God

For the Leader; Al-tashheth. [A Psalm] of David;
Michtam; when he fled from Saul, in the cave.

Be gracious unto me, O God, be gracious unto me,
    For in Thee hath my soul taken refuge;
    Yea, in the shadow of Thy wings will I take refuge,
    Until calamities be overpast.
I will cry unto God Most high;
    Unto God that accomplisheth it for me.
He will send from heaven, and save me,
    When he that would swallow me up taunteth,

                                                    Selah

    God shall send forth His mercy and His truth.
My soul is among lions, I do lie down
        among them that are aflame;
    Even the sons of men, whose teeth
        are spears and arrows,
    And their tongue a sharp sword.

Be Thou exalted, O God, above the heavens;
Thy glory be above all the earth.
They have prepared a net for my steps,
My soul is bowed down;
They have digged a pit before me,
They are fallen into the midst thereof themselves.

Selah

My heart is stedfast, O God, my heart is stedfast;
I will sing, yea, I will sing praises.
Awake, my glory; awake, psaltery and harp;
I will awake the dawn.
I will give thanks unto Thee, O Lord,
among the peoples;
I will sing praises unto Thee among the nations.
For Thy mercy is great unto the heavens,
And Thy truth unto the skies.
Be Thou exalted, O God, above the heavens;
Thy glory be above all the earth. (Psalm 57)

In this prayer, David is embattled, hiding from a large military force in a cave and seeking God's personal rescue. The backstory is found in 1 Samuel 24. King Saul pursues David with an army of three thousand men to Engedi, where David hides in the back of a cave. Engedi is a small area, and it is inevitable that David and his men will be found. But in this prayer, David cries out to God for mercy and expresses his belief that God will come to his rescue.

David seeks refuge "in the shadow of [God's] wings" until he is free from danger (verse 2). David calls on God by the name *El Elyon,* God Most High (verse 3). This conveys his belief that God is more powerful than kings and armies. Although David sees God as the ruler of the universe, he also believes God will be personal, attentive, and responsive to his individual needs. David believes God will show his abiding love and rescue him (verse 4).

To express his inner struggle with fear, David says, "My soul is among lions" (verse 5). However, by verse 8 David claims, "My heart is steadfast." In these two verses, we might conclude that David, by turning his focus to God, is overcoming the "lions" that lurk around his soul. David appears to be so confident that God will deliver him that he sings to God even in dire circumstances (verses 8–9). He proclaims God's name and faithfulness to all peoples and nations (verses 9–10).

David shares his view that God is personal and attentive to individuals even though he believes God is *El Elyon*, the Most High God. It is for this reason that David, in a life-threatening moment, sings God's praises.

As Isaiah proclaims centuries later, "Sing to the Lord, for he has done glorious things; let this be known to all the world. Shout aloud and sing for joy, people of Zion, for great is the Holy One of Israel among you" (Isaiah 12:5–6, NIV).

It is our duty to praise the Lord of all things, to ascribe greatness to him who formed the world in the beginning, since he has not made us like the nations of other lands, and has not placed us like other families of the earth, since he has not assigned unto us a portion as unto them, nor a lot as unto all their multitude. For we bend the knee and offer worship and thanks before the supreme King of kings, the Holy One, blessed be he, who stretched forth the heavens and laid the foundations of the earth, the seat of whose glory is in the heavens above, and the abode of whose might is in the loftiest heights. He is our God; there is none else: in truth he is our King; there is none besides him; as it is written in his Law, And you shall know this day, and lay it to your heart, that the Lord he is God in heaven above and upon the earth beneath: there is none else.

We therefore hope in you, O Lord our God, that we may speedily behold the glory of your might, when you will remove the abominations from the earth, and the idols will be utterly cut off, when the world will be perfected under the kingdom of the Almighty, and all the children of flesh will call upon your name, when you will turn unto yourself all the wicked of the earth. Let all the inhabitants of the world perceive and know that unto you every knee must bow, every tongue must swear. Before you, O Lord our God, let them bow and fall; and unto your glorious name let them give honor; let them all accept the yoke of your kingdom, and reign over them speedily, and for ever and ever. For the kingdom is yours, and to all eternity you will reign in glory; as it is written in your Law, The Lord shall reign for ever and ever. And it is said, And the Lord shall be king over all the earth: in that day shall the Lord be One, and his name One. Amen.

Repairing the Breach

*For the Leader; upon Shushan Eduth; Michtam of
David, to teach; when he strove with Aram-naharaim and
with Aram-zobah, and Joab returned, and smote of Edom
in the Valley of Salt twelve thousand.*

*O God, Thou hast cast us off, Thou
hast broken us down;
Thou hast been angry; O restore us.
Thou hast made the land to shake,
Thou hast cleft it;
Heal the breaches thereof; for it tottereth.
Thou hast made Thy people to see hard things;
Thou hast made us to drink the wine of staggering.
Thou hast given a banner to them that fear Thee,
That it may be displayed because of the truth.*

Selah

That Thy beloved may be delivered,
  Save with Thy right hand, and answer me.

God spoke in His holiness, that I would exult;
  That I would divide Shechem, and
    mete out the valley of Succoth.
Gilead is mine, and Manasseh is mine;
  Ephraim also is the defence of my head;
  Judah is my sceptre.
Moab is my washpot;
  Upon Edom do I cast my shoe;
  Philistia, cry aloud because of me!

Who will bring me into the fortified city?
  Who will lead me unto Edom?
Hast not Thou, O God, cast us off?
  And Thou goest not forth, O God, with our hosts.
Give us help against the adversary;
  For vain is the help of man.
Through God we shall do valiantly;
  For He it is that will tread down our
    adversaries. (Psalm 60)

At the beginning of this prayer, David reflects on his belief that God must be angry with him and his armies. His defenses have been broken, and a seismic rift has occurred in his kingdom. Although an actual earthquake might have occurred, most likely David is describing the crisis as if it were an earthquake that symbolically fractures the kingdom. He asks God to "heal the breaches" (verse 4).

Using a metaphor, David compares the hardship he is facing to wine that makes his people stagger (verse 5). He is afraid that his current situation is a sign of God's rejection, that God no longer assists his armies (verse 12). And so, David prays for God's help. He asks God to restore him and his people (verse 3). He believes only God—not people or armies or rulers—can bring victory (verses 13–14). This belief is reflected in Psalm 146:3: "Do not put your trust in princes, in human beings, who cannot save" (NIV). We can imagine how defeated David must have felt about the thought of not having God's help in his battles.

In the middle of this prayer, David remembers his belief that God is sovereign over the events of nations. He knows God will ultimately "tread down" his enemies and give him victory over them (verse 14). He recalls God's promise that David will victoriously "divide" the regions of Shechem, the valley of Succoth, Gilead and Manasseh, Ephraim, Judah, Moab, and Philistia (verses 8–10).

David's heartfelt prayer reflects his struggles, fears, and resolutions. While David cries out to God and pleads for help, he also expresses his view that God is actively engaged and transcendent over the nations. The writer of Psalm 47 offers a similar perspective: "The nobles of the nations assemble as the people of the God of Abraham, for the kings of the earth belong to God; he is greatly exalted" (verse 9, NIV).

As in David's time, we live in a world fractured by hatred and violence. In our own moments of crisis and confusion, we can perhaps find comfort and courage in the promise of help found in David's prayer in Psalm 60: "Through God we shall do valiantly; for He it is that will tread down our adversaries" (verse 14).

PRAYER

Grant abundant peace unto Israel your people forever; for you are the sovereign Lord of all peace. May it be good in your sight to bless your people Israel at all times and in every hour with your peace.

Baruch Atah Adonai, blessed are you, O Lord, who blesses your people Israel with peace. May he who makes peace in his heaven grant peace to us and to all humanity. Amen.

Dwelling with God

For the Leader; with string-music. [A Psalm] of David.

Hear my cry, O God;
Attend unto my prayer.
From the end of the earth will I call unto Thee,
when my heart fainteth;
Lead me to a rock that is too high for me.
For Thou hast been a refuge for me,
A tower of strength in the face of the enemy.

I will dwell in Thy Tent for ever;
I will take refuge in the covert of Thy wings.

Selah

For Thou, O God, hast heard my vows;
Thou hast granted the heritage of
those that fear Thy name.
Mayest Thou add days unto the king's days!
May his years be as many generations!

May he be enthroned before God for ever!
Appoint mercy and truth, that they may preserve him.

So will I sing praise unto Thy name for ever,
That I may daily perform my vows. (Psalm 61)

Accoording to Jewish scholars, David composed this
short prayer while he was on the run from either Saul
(1 Samuel 19) or his rebellious son Absalom (2 Samuel 15).
When reading this prayer, we can sense the intensity of
David's emotions—the pain, fear, and sorrow he expresses
over the betrayal of a loved one.

First, David asks God to hear him, to take notice of his
plight. Living like a refugee, he feels as though he is at the
"end of the earth" (verse 3), distant from home. His heart is
faint—he is tired, depressed, weak, and fearful. In this condition, he recognizes that self-help will not work. He asks
God to lead him to "a rock that is too high for" him (verse
3). The words of verse 4 indicate that he has already experienced God as his "refuge" and as his "tower of strength in
the face of the enemy." And now he's asking God to let him
"dwell" in that refuge—in God himself—forever (verse 5).

The image of a tent in verse 5 refers to David's feeling of protection under God's care. According to Hebrew
scholars, the term "Tent" here means "your camp" or "under your wing." The line "I will dwell in Thy Tent for ever"

can be seen as an expression of David's longing for a close relationship with God. This type of longing is expressed by other biblical writers besides David. For example, the author of Psalm 42:1–2 writes, "As a deer pants for flowing streams, so pants my soul for you, O God. My soul thirsts for God, for the living God" (ESV).

In addition to providing a description of David's personal needs and longings, the same emotional passion found in Psalm 61 can be seen centuries later when the people of Israel would be carried into exile under Babylonian rule. Speaking through the prophet Ezekiel, God assures the people of Israel: "Although I sent them far away among the nations and scattered them among the countries, yet for a little while I have been a sanctuary for them in the countries where they have gone" (Ezekiel 11:16, NIV).

In verses 6 and 9, David refers to his vows. In the Jewish tradition, vows are much more than promises. They are binding commitments to God that can only be released through a legal process (Numbers 30:1–3). Therefore, when David vows to serve God, he binds himself to God. In Psalm 22:25, David says he publicly offers praise in fulfillment of his vows: "From you comes the theme of my praise in the great assembly; before those who fear you I will fulfill my vows" (NIV).

In verses 7 and 8, David seems to pray for himself in the third person. In this unusual sentence construction, David asks God that the king may have his life extended through "many generations" and that he be preserved by God's "mercy and truth." In David's case, it is likely that this prayer is a plea for life and mercy in the face of exile and death.

However, these lines could also refer to a descendant of David. "Behold, the days are coming, declares the LORD, when I will raise up for David a righteous Branch, and he shall reign as king and deal wisely, and shall execute justice and righteousness in the land. In his days Judah will be saved, and Israel will dwell securely. And this is the name by which he will be called: 'The LORD is our righteousness' " (Jeremiah 23:5–6, ESV; compare Isaiah 11:2).

There are a variety of different ideas about the identity of this descendant. Many Jews believe in a messiah who will come at the end of time, return the Jews to Israel, and rebuild the temple. This descendant of David, according to this tradition, will rule over a world without sorrow, illness, or death.

Other people believe in the coming of a messianic age, a time when all humanity will put aside hatred, prejudice, and violence in favor of world peace. The prophet Isaiah envisions a world where "the wolf shall dwell with the lamb" and "the nursing child shall play over the hole of a cobra," and where "the earth shall be full of the knowledge of the LORD" (Isaiah 11:6–9, ESV).

PRAYER

Av HaRachamim, Father of mercy, sound the great horn for our freedom; lift up the flag to gather our exiles, and gather us from the four corners of the earth. Blessed are you, O Lord, who gathers the banished ones of your people Israel.

Restore our judges as at the first, and our counselors as at the beginning; remove from us grief and suffering; reign over us, O Lord, you alone, in loving-kindness and tender mercy, and justify us in judgment. Blessed are you, O Lord, the King who loves righteousness and judgment.

And to Jerusalem, your city, return in mercy, and dwell there as you have spoken; rebuild it soon in our days as an everlasting building, and speedily set up the throne of David there. Blessed are you, O Lord, who rebuilds Jerusalem.

Speedily cause the offspring of David, your servant, to flourish, and let his horn be exalted by your salvation, because we wait for your salvation all the day. Blessed are you, O Lord, who causes the horn of salvation to flourish.

Hear our voice, O Lord our God; spare us and have mercy upon us, and accept our prayer in mercy and favor; for you are a God who listens to prayers and supplications: from your presence, O our King, turn us not empty away; for you listen in mercy to the prayer of your people Israel. Blessed are you, O Lord, who listens to our prayer.

Rain in the Desert

For the Leader. A Psalm of David, a Song.

Let God arise, let His enemies be scattered;
And let them that hate Him flee before Him.
As smoke is driven away, so drive them away;
As wax melteth before the fire,
So let the wicked perish at the presence of God.
But let the righteous be glad, let them exult before God;
Yea, let them rejoice with gladness.

Sing unto God, sing praises to His name;
Extol Him that rideth upon the skies,
whose name is the LORD;
And exult ye before Him.
A father of the fatherless, and a judge of the widows,
Is God in His holy habitation.
God maketh the solitary to dwell in a house;
He bringeth out the prisoners into prosperity;
The rebellious dwell but in a parched land.

O God, when Thou wentest forth before Thy people,
When Thou didst march through the wilderness;

Selah

The earth trembled, the heavens also
dropped at the presence of God;
Even yon Sinai trembled at the presence
of God, the God of Israel.
A bounteous rain didst Thou pour down, O God;
When Thine inheritance was weary,
Thou didst confirm it.
Thy flock settled therein;
Thou didst prepare in Thy goodness for the
poor, O God. (Psalm 68:1–11)

I n the book of Psalms, David includes prayers and songs written to commemorate specific events in Israel's history. Around those events, David weaves a narrative of God's might and mercy.

Psalm 68 was most likely written to commemorate the reception of the ark of the covenant into Jerusalem (2 Samuel 6). The ark represents the dwelling of God among the people of Israel and serves as a sign of strength and inspiration. From the time of the ark's construction, it is seen as central to many miracles, including the defeat of Jericho by Joshua's army (Joshua 6).

In Psalm 68:1–3, David describes the enemies of God fleeing before him in battle. They are blown away as if they are nothing but smoke in the wind, and they perish as wax melts near a flame.

David changes his focus in verses 4 and 5 to the celebration of those who worship God. In contrast to those who do evil (and therefore dread the presence of God), David describes the exultation, jubilance, singing, and gladness of people who revere God. In verse 5, David calls on his readers to share his elation, to sing to the God who "rideth upon the skies."

David's prayer continues with a rich description of God leading his people through the Sinai. David writes that God brings abundant rain in this dry land, which restores his people and provides for the needy (verses 8–11). Through these words David conveys not only his belief in God's control over nature but also his view of God's personal and compassionate nature.

David then turns his attention to God's concern for people in need. He presents God as not only a great king but also a father who cares for his children. David says God is a father to orphans and a protector of widows (verse 6), a God who is concerned for the homeless and who restores prisoners to a livelihood (verse 7).

Looking at the psalm as a whole, it's possible to see David expressing his view of two aspects of God's nature—his power and judgment over evil, and his love and compassion for the humble. David says that those who turn away from God end up in "a parched land" (verse 7). But those who worship him find an "inheritance" (verse 10) and "salvation" (verse 20).

Every year in the fall, Jews recite a prayer for rain. They ask God to provide enough food to feed everyone, no matter whether they are rich or poor. This psalm, like the prayers of the Jews, can inspire us to participate with God in the care of those in need—those who hunger as well as the widows, orphans, prisoners, and homeless.

PRAYER (THE OPEN SIDDUR PROJECT)

Bless upon us, O Eternal our God, this year and all kinds of its produce for goodness, and bestow dew and rain for blessing on all the face of the earth; and make abundant the face of the world and fulfill the whole of your goodness. Fill our hands with your blessings and the richness of the gifts of your hands.

Preserve and save this year from all evil and from all kinds of destroyers and from all sorts of punishments: and establish for it good hope and as its outcome peace. Spare it and have mercy upon it and all of its harvest and its fruits, and bless it with rains of favor, blessing, and generosity; and let its issue be life, plenty, and peace as in the blessed good years; for you, O Eternal, are good and do good and blesses the years. Blessed be you, O Eternal, who blesses the years.

The God Who Listens

A Prayer of David.

Incline Thine ear, O LORD, and answer me;
*   For I am poor and needy.*
Keep my soul, for I am godly;
*   O Thou my God, save Thy servant that trusteth in Thee.*
Be gracious unto me, O Lord;
*   For unto Thee do I cry all the day.*
Rejoice the soul of Thy servant;
*   For unto Thee, O Lord, do I lift up my soul.*
For Thou, Lord, art good, and ready to pardon,
*   And plenteous in mercy unto all*
*   them that call upon Thee.*

Give ear, O LORD, unto my prayer;
*   And attend unto the voice of my supplications.*
In the day of my trouble I call upon Thee;
*   For Thou wilt answer me.*
There is none like unto Thee among the gods, O Lord,

And there are no works like Thine.
All nations whom Thou hast made shall come
    and prostrate themselves before Thee, O Lord;
  And they shall glorify Thy name.
For Thou art great, and doest wondrous things;
  Thou art God alone.

Teach me, O LORD, Thy way, that I
    may walk in Thy truth;
  Make one my heart to fear Thy name.
I will thank Thee, O Lord my God, with my whole heart;
  And I will glorify Thy name for evermore.
For great is Thy mercy toward me;
  And Thou hast delivered my soul from
    the lowest nether-world.

O God, the proud are risen up against me,
  And the company of violent men
    have sought after my soul,
  And have not set Thee before them.
But Thou, O Lord, art a God full of
    compassion and gracious,
  Slow to anger, and plenteous in mercy and truth.
O turn unto me, and be gracious unto me;
  Give Thy strength unto Thy servant,
  And save the son of Thy handmaid.
Work in my behalf a sign for good;
  That they that hate me may see it, and be put to shame,

Because Thou, LORD, hast helped me,
and comforted me. (Psalm 86)

W ill you please just listen to me?" That plea is made daily in homes, schools, workplaces, and businesses. It might be an unspoken plea, such as when we tap "mute" on the remote, or it can be a blatant request like when a child tugs on a parent's sleeve and says repeatedly, "Daddy, Daddy, Daddy."

When David is threatened by "violent" enemies (verse 14)—whether other nations seeking to overthrow Israel or traitors within his own kingdom—he pleads with God, "Incline Thine ear" (verse 1). He appears to be blatantly asking God, "Lean down and listen to me!" His prayer in Psalm 86 gives us an inside view of the closeness between God and David. David relies on God to hear his plea and to save him.

David calls himself "poor and needy" (verse 1). His prayer is the cry of a servant, *'eved,* to his lord, *'adon.* In ancient culture, an *'eved* belonged to an *'adon* and lived under that lord's authority, support, and protection. In describing himself as God's "servant" (verses 2, 4, 16) and "the son of [God's] handmaid" (verse 16), David places himself in the lowest position, as a bonded slave. He literally sees himself as indentured to God for life. His words suggest that to be the servant of God can be seen as a high honor, not the lowest state of being.

David prays for God to preserve his life and bring him joy. His confidence in prayer may come from what he believes about God's character (verses 5, 15). In verse 15, David calls God *Eloheynu Mayrachaim*, a God "full of compassion." This verse quotes Exodus 24:6, where God proclaims his name to Moses (see also Psalms 103:8 and 145:8). David's soul seems to be calmed with the reality of God's goodness, even in his time of trouble.

Additionally, David's confidence in prayer may rest on what he believes about God's incomparable greatness and deity (verse 8). The composer of Psalm 115 shares similar views in speaking disparagingly of other nations' gods: "Their idols are silver and gold, the work of human hands. They have mouths, but do not speak; eyes, but do not see. They have ears, but do not hear; noses, but do not smell. They have hands, but do not feel; feet, but do not walk; and they do not make a sound in their throat" (verses 4–7, ESV). In Psalm 86, David tells God that his matchless deeds will cause the whole world to acknowledge Israel's God as the one true God (verses 8, 10), a prominent theme in the Bible (Exodus 7:5; 1 Samuel 17:46; 1 Kings 8:41–43; Psalms 22:27–29, 66:1–7; Ezekiel 20:41).

David prays for God to deliver him from not just his enemies but also his own divided heart (verse 11). He wants to be wholeheartedly devoted to God (verse 12). This kind of devotion fulfills God's command in Deuteronomy 6:5: "Love the LORD your God with all your heart and with all your soul and with all your strength" (NIV).

Throughout Psalm 86 David repeatedly pleads with God to listen to him and to give him mercy (verses 1–3, 6, 16). He concludes his prayer with a note of confidence that God has granted him help and comfort (verse 17). He asks for a sign of God's favor as a way to frustrate those who set themselves up as enemies against him (verse 17).

This psalm can offer inspiration for finding hope in the midst of any of life's hardships. We can consider how David experienced the personal attention of God as he humbled himself and prayed for God to grant him mercy, deliverance, and strength.

Psalm 86 promotes worship of, and prayer to, God alone. In our time, many gods of the biblical era are no longer worshiped, but plenty of gods, or idols, still exist. Some people worship the god of money or the god of power. For some, technology can be an idol. The list is long of gods that "have ears, but do not hear." David's words in this psalm encourage us to pray wholeheartedly to a God who bends down and listens to us.

PRAYER

Shema koleinu adonai eloheinu, chus verachem aleinu, vekabel berachamim uvratzon et tefilateinu.

Hear our voice, O Lord our God; spare us and have mercy upon us, and accept our prayer in mercy and favor. Amen.

Music of the Soul

A Song. A Psalm of David.

My heart is steadfast, O God;
  I will sing, yea, I will sing praises,
    even with my glory.
Awake, psaltery and harp;
  I will awake the dawn.
I will give thanks unto Thee, O LORD, among the peoples;
  And I will sing praises unto Thee among the nations.
For Thy mercy is great above the heavens,
  And Thy truth reacheth unto the skies.
Be Thou exalted, O God, above the heavens;
  And Thy glory be above all the earth.
That Thy beloved may be delivered,
  Save with Thy right hand, and answer me.

God spoke in His holiness, that I would exult;
  That I would divide Shechem, and
    mete out the valley of Succoth.

Gilead is mine, Manasseh is mine;
    Ephraim also is the defence of my head;
    Judah is my sceptre.
Moab is my washpot;
    Upon Edom do I cast my shoe;
    Over Philistia do I cry aloud.
Who will bring me into the fortified city?
    Who will lead me unto Edom?
Hast not Thou cast us off, O God?
    And Thou goest not forth, O God, with our hosts?
Give us help against the adversary;
    For vain is the help of man.
Through God we shall do valiantly;
    For He it is that will tread down our
        adversaries. (Psalm 108)

Why do we sing? Why listen to music as we drive, exercise, and work? Perhaps you are listening to music as you read this devotion. Why spend time and money to attend musical performances? One reason is because, for many, music reaches deep into our souls and expresses what words alone cannot say.

Perhaps David, described as "the hero of Israel's songs" (2 Samuel 23:1, NIV), composed and sang songs because music best expressed his heartfelt desires, fears, joys, and sorrows.

The superscription of Psalm 108 designates this prayer of David as a song or a poem. (The Hebrew term שִׁיר can mean "a poem" or "a song.") It is a compilation of two other psalms (called a remix in today's vernacular): verses 2–6 correspond with Psalm 57:8–11, while verses 7–14 echo Psalm 60:7–14.

If we listen with ears of imagination, we may hear a melody of reverent joy as David declares he will sing praises to God with his entire being. As David sings, he most likely accompanies himself with a harp or lyre (verse 3; see 1 Samuel 16:14–23). These stringed instruments, slightly different in size and formation, were used in Israel's worship celebrations (2 Samuel 6:5; Psalm 150).

Implied in this psalm is that David awakens before sunrise with a song of praise on his lips (verses 2–3). He doesn't seem shy about singing praises to God, for he proposes to do so among all nations and peoples (verse 4). He is "steadfast" (verse 2) about making music to God— his mind is firm on the matter.

David's song expresses his conviction that God's love and faithfulness are greater than this earth's vast firmament. He vocalizes how God, whose love he believes reaches higher than the skies, is elevated "above the heavens" (verse 6).

We can almost hear the percussive beat grow stronger in the next stanza as David recounts how he believes God saved the people of Israel in the past and will continue to do so in the future. In verse 7 David asks God to help the people with his "right hand," a figure of speech referring to God's saving power (Psalms 17:7, 20:7, 89:14), protection and presence (Psalm 16:8, 11), and victory (Exodus 15:6; Psalm 44:3–4).

David poetically portrays God as a warrior-king who pronounces dominion over territories of the tribes of Jacob (Joshua 13–19). Shechem, the Valley of Sukkoth, Gilead, and Manasseh (verses 8–9) represent regions west and east of the Jordan River in David's kingdom of Judah.

Psalm 108 highlights two prominent tribes of Israel. Ephraim was allotted hill country in the north (Joshua 19:50, 24:30). David describes Ephraim as "the defence of [his] head" (verse 9), symbolizing this tribe's force and military strength (Deuteronomy 33:17). Judah's territory was in the southern portion of Canaan. When Jacob blessed his sons, he pronounced, "The scepter shall not depart from Judah" (Genesis 49:10, ESV), giving this tribe the right to rule. King David and his successors were from the line of Judah.

God's victory over Israel's long-standing enemies of Moab, Edom, and Philistia—symbolized by David's description of God washing his feet in Moab and tossing his sandal on Edom (verse 10)—signifies to David that God will "tread down" Israel's enemies (verse 14).

If we were listening to this song being performed (although we don't know the tune or meter), perhaps we would hear the musicians transition to a minor key as David laments his sense that God no longer marches with

Israel's armies into battle. David's questions are possibly intended to induce God to positive action on behalf of Israel. With the words "vain is the help of man" (verse 13), David reveals his view that human alliances and might are worthless but God's intervention is essential for victory. This view is repeated often by writers of the Bible (Psalms 20:7–8, 118:8, 124:1–3, 146:3–5; Isaiah 30:1–5).

David concludes his song with a refrain of faith and triumph, expressing confidence that God's punishment of Israel is only temporary. His words convey certainty that God will once again lead Israel victoriously into battle.

Psalm 108 can propel us to recognize the power of music and harness its potential to do good in our lives. David shared his heartfelt beliefs, fears, and desires through prayers and songs. Perhaps meaningful expressions through music can motivate us to live in light of our own convictions.

PRAYER

The Hymn of Glory

I will chant sweet hymns and compose songs; for my soul longs for you.

My soul desires to be beneath the shadow of your hand, to know all your secret mysteries.

Even while I speak of your glory, my
heart yearns for your love.

Therefore will I speak glorious things of you, and
will honor your name with songs of love.

I will declare your glory, though I have
never seen you; I describe your name,
though I have not known you.

The sum of your word is truth; you, who have
called every generation from the beginning,
seek the people that look for you.

Accept, I beg you, my many songs, and let
my joyous words come to you.

Let my praise be a crown upon your head, and
my prayer rise to you like incense.

Let the song of the poor be precious in your sight like
the song that was sung at your sacrifices.

May my blessing rise to the bountiful God, who
creates and produces, who is just and mighty.

May my meditation be pleasant to you,
for my soul longs for you.

A Calmed and Quieted Soul

A Song of Ascents; of David.

LORD, my heart is not haughty, nor mine eyes lofty;
  Neither do I exercise myself in things too great,
    or in things too wonderful for me.
Surely I have stilled and quieted my soul;
  Like a weaned child with his mother;
  My soul is with me like a weaned child.

O Israel, hope in the LORD
  From this time forth and for ever. (Psalm 131)

P salms 120–134 are a compilation of fifteen psalms
 bearing the superscription "A Song of Ascents." It
is theorized these songs were sung as pilgrims journeyed

to Jerusalem for the three annual festivals of *Pesach* (Passover), *Sukkot* (the Feast of Tabernacles), and *Shavuot* (the Feast of Weeks) in obedience to God's command in Deuteronomy 16:16: "Three times a year all your males shall appear before the LORD your God at the place that he will choose: at the Feast of Unleavened Bread, at the Feast of Weeks, and at the Feast of Booths. They shall not appear before the LORD empty-handed" (ESV).

According to Jewish scholars, however, these fifteen psalms were sung specifically by the Levites when they descended the fifteen steps going down from one temple area to another. They sang the words of these psalms to affirm God's blessings and protection on the people of Israel. The Hebrew word translated by the English *ascent* (*ma'aloth*) means "steps or stages." No matter what direction travelers were coming from, they spoke of going "up" to Jerusalem (1 Kings 12:28; Psalm 122:3–4; Isaiah 2:3).

These fifteen psalms contain metaphors familiar to the people who sang them: sowing and reaping (Psalm 126), arrows in a quiver (Psalm 127), fruitful vines and olive shoots (Psalm 128), plowed furrows (Psalm 129), anointing oil and refreshing dew (Psalm 133).

Psalm 131, one of four songs of ascent credited to David (along with Psalms 122, 124, and 133), reflects a scene every pilgrim would have been familiar with—that of a young child resting happily in its mother's arms. In this very brief psalm, David makes a statement of humility, paints a picture of trust, and issues a call for hope.

In the first verse of his prayer David rejects a proud, haughty attitude that lifts up its heart, presuming to be God (Ezekiel 28:2–6), and that raises its eyes, assuming superiority over others (Proverbs 30:13). Biblical writers, including David, often wrote about how God despises pride and values humility (2 Samuel 22:28; Psalms 101:5, 138:6; Proverbs 6:16–17; Isaiah 2:12; Zephaniah 3:11).

David, like all of us, was often confronted with deep questions about life. In declaring that he does not occupy himself with "things too wonderful" (verse 1), he most likely isn't saying he chooses to be shallow. Rather, he seems to agree with Moses that "the secret things belong to the LORD our God" (Deuteronomy 29:29, ESV). His words suggest he recognizes that some mysteries of God are beyond his understanding (see Isaiah 55:8–9). Rather than arrogantly speaking for God like one who knows as much as God, David seems to express a humble willingness to answer some of life's hardest questions with "I don't know." We can conclude that David determines to trust God even though he doesn't always understand God's ways.

Instead of haughtily assuming the role of God, or getting upset because he doesn't understand God, David calms down and quiets his soul (verse 2). David seems to calm himself by trusting in God's wisdom. His choice echoes the prayer of Psalm 116:7: "Return, O my soul, to your rest; for the LORD has dealt bountifully with you" (ESV).

David uses the simile of a "weaned child" (verse 2) to poetically portray his relationship with God. Infants who nurse may be fussy when held against their mother's breast because they want to be fed. David's picture of a weaned child at peace, not demanding or discontented but simply happy to be with its mother, describes his own sense of contentment, peace, and tranquility in God's presence.

David concludes his song with a call to hope in God (verse 3). The previous song of ascent states why God's people can hope in him: "O Israel, hope in the Lord! For with the Lord there is steadfast love, and with him is plentiful redemption" (Psalm 130:7, ESV).

Psalm 131 is a calm oasis in a world of hurried frenzy. Much like Shabbat, the Sabbath, it invites us to stop and rest—to cease the rushing that accompanies our need to always be "doing" and instead experience contentment in simply "being." That is why on the Sabbath, we forego our daily routine and stop to listen to God's voice without distraction. The world insists we earn significance by what we accomplish; Psalm 131 perhaps suggests the greatest accomplishment is humbly trusting God and enjoying his presence, which is why the observance of the Shabbat is one of Judaism's most important commandments.

David's song of ascent also urges us to be content to live within the mystery. Rather than overworking ourselves trying to explain a God who cannot be fully comprehended, we can make the conscious choice to trust God with our unanswered questions and put our hope in him.

PRAYER

Be pleased, O Lord our God, to strengthen us by your commandments, and especially by the commandment of the seventh day, this great and holy Sabbath, since this day is great and holy before you, that we may rest and renew ourselves in love in accordance with your will. In your favor, O Lord our God, grant that there be no trouble, grief, or lamenting on the day of our rest. Let us, O Lord our God, behold the consolation of Zion and the rebuilding of Jerusalem your holy city, for you are the Lord of salvation and rest.

Eloheinu v'Elohei Avoteinu, our God and God of our ancestors, accept our rest; sanctify us by your commandments, and grant our portion in your Law; satisfy us with your goodness, and bring us joy with your salvation; purify our hearts to serve you in truth; and in your love and favor, O Lord our God, let us inherit the holy Sabbath; and may Israel, who blesses your name, rest on that day. Praised are you, O Lord, who makes holy the Sabbath day. Amen.

Wholehearted Living

[A Psalm] of David.

I will give Thee thanks with my whole heart,
In the presence of the mighty will
I sing praises unto Thee.
I will bow down toward Thy holy temple,
And give thanks unto Thy name for
Thy mercy and for Thy truth;
For Thou hast magnified Thy word
above all Thy name.
In the day that I called, Thou didst answer me;
Thou didst encourage me in my soul with strength.

All the kings of the earth shall give Thee thanks, O LORD,
For they have heard the words of Thy mouth.
Yea, they shall sing of the ways of the LORD;
For great is the glory of the LORD.

*For though the L*ORD *be high, yet*
regardeth He the lowly,
And the haughty He knoweth from afar.
Though I walk in the midst of trouble,
Thou quickenest me;
Thou stretchest forth Thy hand against
the wrath of mine enemies,
And Thy right hand doth save me.
*The L*ORD *will accomplish that which concerneth me;*
*Thy mercy, O L*ORD*, endureth for ever;*
Forsake not the work of Thine own
hands. (Psalm 138)

A trial septal defect (ASD) is a congenital heart defect commonly known as a hole in the heart. If the hole between the upper chambers of the heart does not close on its own, surgery is needed to repair the defect. If not repaired, a hole in the heart will eventually result in extreme fatigue, damaged heart and lungs, and possibly a shorter life span. David, who never presents himself as a half-hearted kind of person in his prayers, would probably say that a whole, healthy heart is just as important in the spiritual realm as it is in the physical.

In Psalm 138 David offers God a prayer of thanksgiving for his help and salvation. This psalm contains distinctive features that identify it as an individual thanksgiving psalm:

a declaration of thanksgiving, a reason for thanksgiving, a summons to praise, and an expression of confidence in God.

David declares his gratitude with his "whole heart" (verse 1), putting everything he has into thanking and praising God. He sings without reservation "in the presence of the mighty" (verse 1). Here the word "mighty" can refer to gods, angels, idols, or rulers of pagan nations. David agrees with other psalmists who declare, "For the LORD is a great God, and a great King above all gods" (Psalm 95:3, ESV) and "For all the gods of the peoples are worthless idols, but the LORD made the heavens" (Psalm 96:5, ESV).

David adds a physical action to his wholehearted worship—he bows down toward the temple (verse 2). Since no temple existed when David was king, it is conjectured he was referring to the tent where the ark of God resided (2 Samuel 6:17). According to the biblical record, David's son Solomon was privileged to construct a magnificent temple for God (1 Kings 6). At its dedication Solomon acknowledged a physical temple cannot contain God. He marveled that God said of the temple, "My name shall be there," and he prayed that God would listen to his people "when they pray toward this place" (1 Kings 8:29–30, ESV). We can conclude that David isn't so much bowing toward a place but toward the holy presence of God.

David acknowledges God's *chesed*, his covenantal, loyal love (verse 2). He responds to God's love and faithfulness with gratitude. David then states the reason for his thanksgiving. He apparently had been in a distressful situation, but when he called to God, God poured strength into his soul (verse 3). And David points out in his prayer that God answers him "in the day" he calls to God (verse 3). God's response to David in the context of this prayer is without delay. This attentiveness from God would give David even more reason for expressing his wholehearted gratitude to God.

David's words in this psalm convey his view that God's steadfast love and faithfulness toward him are a powerful testimony to the other "kings of the earth" (verse 4). David anticipates a day when those kings will respond to a summons to praise God (verses 4–5). According to various biblical passages, God chose the Israelites to bear perpetual witness to the existence and glory of God so that all nations and peoples will know and praise him (Deuteronomy 4; Psalm 22:27–28; Isaiah 43:9–12).

David seems to be saying that in his specific situation the kings of the earth will praise God for being gracious to the lowly David and for punishing the haughty ones who have caused David distress (verses 4–7). Perhaps God regards "the lowly" (verse 6) because they humbly acknowledge him (Isaiah 57:15) but stays distant from "the haughty" (verse 6) because they have no regard for him (Psalm 10:4).

David concludes by expressing his wholehearted confidence in God. He seems to be well aware that troubles will come, but he trusts God to preserve and protect him in the midst of them (verse 7). He rejoices in his belief that God has a purpose for his life and will fulfill it (verse 8). The declaration "the LORD will accomplish" suggests that David fully expects God to work on his behalf and not "forsake" him (verse 8).

We may find ourselves dragging through our days, tired, unfocused, and soul-weary. It could be that we're living with a spiritual hole in the heart. Psalm 138 can motivate us to wholeheartedness—we can live gratefully, hopefully, humbly, and purposefully.

PRAYER

Eloheinu v'Elohei Avoteinu, our God and God of our ancestors, you are the great Comforter, who gives us shalom, wholeness, and peace. Restore our hearts and heal the brokenhearted. Help us to listen to you and each other, so that we can be the instrument of your light to those in the darkness of grief or loneliness. Let us inspire hope by being attentive to the needs of our fellow human beings and bringing them your healing, as your prophet Isaiah describes:

The Spirit of the Sovereign LORD is on me,
because the LORD has anointed me
to proclaim good news to the poor.
He has sent me to bind up the brokenhearted,
to proclaim freedom for the captives
and release from darkness for the
prisoners. (Isaiah 61:1, NIV)

Amen.

36

Known by God

For the Leader. A Psalm of David.

O LORD, Thou hast searched me, and known me.
Thou knowest my downsitting and mine uprising,
    Thou understandest my thought afar off.
Thou measurest my going about and my lying down,
    And art acquainted with all my ways.
For there is not a word in my tongue,
    But, lo, O LORD, Thou knowest it altogether.
Thou hast hemmed me in behind and before,
    And laid Thy hand upon me.
Such knowledge is too wonderful for me;
    Too high, I cannot attain unto it.

Whither shall I go from Thy spirit?
    Or whither shall I flee from Thy presence?
If I ascend up into heaven, Thou art there;
    If I make my bed in the nether-world, behold,
        Thou art there.

If I take the wings of the morning,
    And dwell in the uttermost parts of the sea;
Even there would Thy hand lead me,
    And Thy right hand would hold me.
And if I say: "Surely the darkness shall envelop me,
    And the light about me shall be night";
Even the darkness is not too dark for Thee,
    But the night shineth as the day;
    The darkness is even as the light.

For Thou hast made my reins;
    Thou hast knit me together in my mother's womb.
I will give thanks unto Thee,
        for I am fearfully and wonderfully made;
    Wonderful are Thy works; and that
        my soul knoweth right well.
My frame was not hidden from Thee,
    When I was made in secret,
    And curiously wrought
        in the lowest parts of the earth.
Thine eyes did see mine unformed substance,
    And in Thy book they were all written—
    Even the days that were fashioned,
    When as yet there was none of them.
How weighty also are Thy thoughts unto me, O God!
    How great is the sum of them!
If I would count them, they are more
        in number than the sand;

Were I to come to the end of them, I
would still be with Thee.

If Thou but wouldest slay the wicked, O God—
Depart from me therefore, ye men of blood;
Who utter Thy name with wicked thought,
They take it for falsehood, even Thine enemies—
Do not I hate them, O LORD, that hate Thee?
And do not I strive with those
that rise up against Thee?
I hate them with utmost hatred;
I count them mine enemies.
Search me, O God, and know my heart,
Try me, and know my thoughts;
And see if there be any way in me that is grievous,
And lead me in the way everlasting. (Psalm 139)

In Psalm 139 David marvels at God's deep knowledge of him and God's love for him. Although David does not use the word *love* in this prayer, he implies God's love for him in his descriptions of God's care for him in everything he does and everywhere he goes. This psalm is an intensely personal reflection on God's omniscience (he knows everything), omnipresence (he is everywhere), and omnipotence (he possesses all power.)

In this prayer, David seems to fully believe that God knows everything about him—his actions, travels, habits, quirks, words, thoughts, and motives (verses 1–4). David doesn't appear horrified that God knows him so intimately; rather, his words convey the safety and comfort he feels as he is encircled within God's powerful hand of protection and blessing (verse 5).

David's prayer suggests he believes God is everywhere, reigning sovereign over all creation (verses 7–10). In saying, "Wither shall I flee from Thy presence?" (verse 7), David most likely is not implying he wants to flee from God; rather, he seems to marvel at the impossibility of escaping God's presence. He cannot hide from God even if he goes to the highest height, deepest depth, darkest night, or the most remote island on the planet. The book of Jeremiah also describes this omnipresent character of God: " 'Who can hide in secret places so that I cannot see them?' declares the LORD. 'Do not I fill heaven and earth?' declares the LORD" (Jeremiah 23:24, NIV). According to some biblical passages, even Sheol, the realm of the dead, lies exposed before God (Job 26:6; Amos 9:2). Rather than feeling stifled or resentful, David appears grateful for God's constant guiding and sustaining presence.

In David's understanding, God's incomparable knowledge, presence, and power extend to the womb (verse 13). He believes God fashioned his unique physical and mental attributes and was as personally involved in creating every aspect of his being as a knitter casting every stitch of a garment (see also Job 10:11; Isaiah 44:24). Perhaps David paused to consider the intricacies of the human body and praised God for such a wonderful work. "Wonderfully made" (verse 14) is a potent term in the Hebrew language that emphasizes God's unrivaled power that creates each person as a unique masterpiece.

David appears to regard himself as a person treasured by God, not just a number or concept to an impersonal deity. He feels a sense of value because he believes, as do other Bible writers, that his name is recorded in God's book (verse 16; see also Exodus 32:32; Psalm 69:28–29). He may also feel a sense of divine purpose that was determined before he was even born, such as God declared to Jeremiah: "Before I formed you in the womb I knew you, before you were born I set you apart; I appointed you as a prophet to the nations" (Jeremiah 1:5, NIV). God's countless thoughts are too magnificent for David to comprehend. What is even more amazing to David is that God's weighty and innumerable thoughts (verses 17–18) are personal, "precious" thoughts concerning him (Psalm 139:17, NIV).

The transition from verse 18 to verse 19 seems rather jarring. In the earlier part of the psalm David expresses his view of a God who masterfully creates and values humans. In verse 19 he voices his desire for God to "slay the wicked." David is speaking of wicked murderers who have no respect for human life, enemies who defy the God whom David loves, enemies "who utter [God's] name with wicked thought" (verse 20). Therefore, David hates them and prays for their demise (verses 21–22).

This sentiment of hating the wicked is repeated often in the Psalms (5:5–7, 11:5, 26:5, 109:6–20).

Psalm 139 doesn't end on this tone of vengeance. David stops despairing over his wicked enemies and brings the focus back to his own heart's posture before God. David concludes the psalm with a request for God to continue searching and knowing him (verses 23–24). He asks God to reveal anything in his life that is offensive to God and to guide him to live in ways that please God. The assurance that God loves and treasures him could be David's underlying motivation for longing to be examined, known, and guided by God.

Psalm 139 calls us to honor God's greatness by valuing his masterpiece of humanity. Perhaps we can follow David's example by asking God to examine our hearts and minds so that our motives and attitudes can please God and positively influence the lives of the people around us.

PRAYER

"He said, 'Can I not do with you, Israel, as this potter does?' declares the Lord. 'Like clay in the hand of the potter, so are you in my hand, Israel' " (Jeremiah 18:6, NIV).

As clay in the hands of the potter, to be shaped as he pleases,

So are we in your hands, Preserver of kindness, to be shaped as you will.

As stone in the hands of the cutter, how he carves or smashes it at his will,

So are we in your hands, Source of life and death,

Remember the covenant and rebuke the Prosecutor.

As silver in the hands of the silversmith, who thickens and thins as he will,

So purify us, heavenly sculptor, remember the covenant and bless us with purity and peace. Amen.

37

Character Sculpting

A Psalm of David.

LORD, *I have called Thee; make haste unto me;*
    Give ear unto my voice, when I call unto Thee.
Let my prayer be set forth as incense before Thee,
    The lifting up of my hands as the evening sacrifice.
Set a guard, O LORD, *to my mouth;*
    Keep watch at the door of my lips.
Incline not my heart to any evil thing,
    To be occupied in deeds of wickedness
    With men that work iniquity;
    And let me not eat of their dainties.

Let the righteous smite me in kindness,
        and correct me;
    Oil so choice let not my head refuse;
    For still is my prayer because of their wickedness.
Their judges are thrown down by the sides of the rock;
    And they shall hear my words, that they are sweet.

As when one cleaveth and breaketh up the earth,
  Our bones are scattered at the grave's mouth.

For mine eyes are unto Thee, O GOD the Lord;
  In Thee have I taken refuge, O pour not out my soul.
Keep me from the snare which they have laid for me,
  And from the gins of the workers of iniquity.
Let the wicked fall into their own nets,
  Whilst I withal escape. (Psalm 141)

In this prayer, David seems to take an honest look at his character. He admits he needs correction from God and righteous people (verses 3–5), and he asks for God to protect him from evil (verses 8–9). He is fearful of falling into "the snare . . . of the workers of iniquity" (verse 9), indicating that he wants to be a man of good character.

In a beautiful example of humility, David prays for correction when he sins. He says he is willing to receive punishment for his character flaws. In asking for correction, David uses strong words: "Let the righteous smite me in kindness, and correct me; oil so choice let not my head refuse" (verse 5).

David lived this principle when he was challenged by the prophet Nathan about his adultery with Bathsheba. When she became pregnant, David sent her husband, Uriah, to the front lines knowing he would not survive the battle (2 Samuel 11). When Nathan confronts David about his sin, he accepts the rebuke, saying, "I have sinned against *Adonai* [the Lord]" (2 Samuel 12:13, CJB).

Many Bible scholars teach that in Psalm 51, David shares his heartfelt confession about what he has done with Bathsheba and to Uriah. While his confession saves his dynasty, he is punished severely. David understands and accepts these consequences. He mourns, but there is no indication that he blames others or is bitter.

David starts his prayer in Psalm 141 by praying for the nearness of God (verse 1). Then, in verse 2, David asks that God count his prayer as an offering of "incense." This is likely an expression of his understanding that sacrifices are merely external rituals and that God is most interested in the true condition of his heart. In Psalm 51:17 he writes, "My sacrifice, O God, is a broken spirit; a broken and contrite heart you, God, will not despise" (NIV).

Looking closely at verse 3, we see that David believes speech is an essential aspect of his character. He prays for purity in his speech. As the book of Proverbs teaches, "The tongue has power over life and death; those who indulge it must eat its fruit" (18:21, CJB).

In David's pursuit of good character, he also prays that God will guide him away from temptation. He expresses his understanding of how peer pressure plays a role in temptation (verse 4). So, David asks God to keep him distant from "men that work iniquity" (verse 4). The author of Psalm 1:1 wrote similar words: "How blessed are those who reject the advice of the wicked, don't stand on the way of sinners or sit where scoffers sit!" (CJB).

Taken as a whole, Psalm 141 can be seen as David's prayer for good moral character. To this end, we can see that he is willing to be corrected by righteous judges and by God. As we reflect on this psalm, we can make sure that our own hearts are willing to humbly accept correction. And perhaps the psalm will give us courage to lovingly encourage and instruct others toward good character, and to protect each other from evil.

As Proverbs 8:33 reminds us, "Hear instruction, and grow wise; do not refuse it" (CJB).

PRAYER

O lead us not into the power of sin, or of transgression or iniquity, or of temptation, or of scorn: let not the evil inclination have sway over us: keep us far from bad companion: make us cleave to the good inclination and to good works: subdue our inclination so that it may submit itself unto you; and let us obtain this day, and every day, grace, favor and mercy in your eyes, and in the eyes of all who behold us; and bestow loving-kindnesses upon us. Blessed are you, O Lord, who bestows loving-kindnesses upon your people Israel.

May it be your will, O Lord my God and God of my fathers, to deliver me this day, and every day, from arrogant people and from arrogance, from a bad companion and from a bad neighbor, and from any mishap, and from the adversary that destroys; from a hard judgment, and from a hard opponent, whether they be offspring of the covenant or be not offspring of the covenant.

A Dark Cave

Maschil of David, when he was in the cave;
a Prayer.

With my voice I cry unto the LORD;
With my voice I make supplication unto the LORD.
I pour out my complaint before Him,
I declare before Him my trouble;
When my spirit fainteth within me—
Thou knowest my path—
In the way wherein I walk
Have they hidden a snare for me.
Look on my right hand, and see,
For there is no man that knoweth me;
I have no way to flee;
No man careth for my soul.

I have cried unto Thee, O LORD;
I have said: "Thou art my refuge,
My portion in the land of the living."

Attend unto my cry;
For I am brought very low;
Deliver me from my persecutors;
For they are too strong for me.
Bring my soul out of prison,
That I may give thanks unto Thy name;
The righteous shall crown themselves because of me;
For Thou wilt deal bountifully with me. (Psalm 142)

William Cowper, a renowned eighteenth-century poet, described a dark time in a letter to his cousin. He wrote: "I am hunted by spiritual hounds in the night season."[5] He goes on to express feelings of being closed in and trapped. God seems distant.

While writing Psalm 142, David is trapped in a dark cave and hunted by deadly enemies. This experience, as seen in the words of his prayer, creates in David emotions of fear, loneliness, and abandonment. David, so overwhelmed by these events, also wrote Psalm 57 while hiding from Saul in the wilderness.

Psalm 142 is so moving and transparent that it is often recited by Jews who are faced with acute danger. Many others find comfort in the psalm when they are emotionally trapped and overwhelmed by life.

---

5   William Cowper, quoted in *The Roots of Sorrow* by Richard Winter (Wheaton, IL: Crossway Books, 1986), 20.

What leads David to hide in the cave is King Saul's tireless effort to kill him. Saul knows that God is removing him and his descendants from the throne and establishing David as king (1 Samuel 18:28–29). David flees Saul and spends years fearing for his life in the wilderness. He ends up hiding from Saul in a cave with only one entrance.

In his anxiety, David cries out to God in this prayer, pleading for mercy. This is no prayer of meditation, which often characterizes David's late-night prayers. In verse 2, David says twice that he is praying aloud, giving voice to his suffering and fear. He pours out his heart to God, not poetically or with forethought, but in a raw, emotional appeal. He says, "I pour out my complaint before Him" (verse 3).

David shares all his feelings with God. As an open book, he says his spirit is failing, he has no friends, he feels alone and confined, and there is no one to care for him (verses 4–5). He is depressed, and his relentless and ruthless enemies are "too strong" for him (verse 7). We can only imagine the doom and ominous dread he must be experiencing in that cold cave.

As we see so often in David's prayers, he shares his heart and then reaches out to God, his only steadfast companion and source of hope. In his desperation, he acknowledges God as his refuge (verse 6). In his humility, David admits he cannot survive without God's help. David asks God to deliver him and to "bring [his] soul out of prison" (verse 8).

Perhaps this prison was not just the cave in which he was hiding but also the chains of despair, hopelessness, and weakness. The physical dangers he faces naturally create spiritual and emotional angst, as this psalm so powerfully displays. We can see that David is a prisoner in the back of the cave, but his soul is also in turmoil. He longs to break free in a spiritual sense, to give thanks, to be in the company of good people, and to experience again God's bounty (verse 9).

Many find comfort in this psalm, perhaps because it demonstrates that even strong and good people sometimes face despair, have doubts, and feel overwhelmed by problems. David is God's chosen leader and the man who defeated Goliath; and yet, he is prone to the same challenges, sorrows, problems, and emotions that are common to most people. And despite David's struggles, he continues to praise God and turn to him for help.

In the stories in the Bible, we read that God used many people who had great weaknesses or suffered immense trials. Noah may have been an alcoholic (Genesis 9:21). Sarah doubted God's promise that she would have a son (Genesis 18). Jacob deceived his father (Genesis 27), lost his most beloved wife, Rachel, in childbirth (Genesis 35), and after many other hardships and tragedies, lost Joseph, his favorite son, to slavery (Genesis 37). Moses, the greatest leader, teacher, and prophet of the Jewish people, was prone to anger (Numbers 20). All of them, like David, were chosen servants of God, and all of them, like David, experienced brokenness and pain.

Many people experience despair, loneliness, and the feeling of being trapped—the same emotions David felt.

David's response, as shown in this psalm, is to pour out his soul to God. He is not ashamed to share everything he feels and thinks. And he asks God to be his refuge and rescuer. It is possible to see this psalm as a profound expression of David's relationship with God, even in terrifying times.

PRAYER

Ribbono Shel Olam (Master of the universe), as for us, we know not what to do, but our eyes are upon you. Remember, O Lord, your tender mercies and loving-kindnesses; for they have been ever of old. Let your loving-kindness, O Lord, be upon us, as we have waited for you. Please don't remember against us the iniquities of our ancestors. Let your tender mercies speedily come to meet us; for we are brought very low. Be gracious unto us, O Lord, be gracious unto us; for we are filled with contempt. Remember to be merciful. You know our frame. You remember that we are dust. Help us, O God of our salvation, for the sake of the glory of your name. Deliver us, and pardon our sins, for your name's sake. Amen.

Avinu Malkeinu, our Father, our King, be gracious unto us and answer us, for we have no good works of our own; deal with us in charity and loving-kindness, and save us.

Beyond the Self

A Psalm of David.

O LORD, *hear my prayer,*
give ear to my supplications;
In Thy faithfulness answer me, and
in Thy righteousness.
And enter not into judgment with Thy servant;
For in Thy sight shall no man living be justified.

For the enemy hath persecuted my soul;
He hath crushed my life down to the ground;
He hath made me to dwell in darkness,
as those that have been long dead.
And my spirit fainteth within me;
My heart within me is appalled.

I remember the days of old;
I meditate on all Thy doing;
I muse on the work of Thy hands.

I spread forth my hands unto Thee;
  My soul [thirsteth] after Thee, as a weary land.

                                        Selah

Answer me speedily, O Lord,
  My spirit faileth;
  Hide not Thy face from me;
  Lest I become like them
    that go down into the pit.
Cause me to hear Thy lovingkindness in the morning,
  For in Thee do I trust;
  Cause me to know the way wherein I should walk,
  For unto Thee have I lifted up my soul.
Deliver me from mine enemies, O Lord;
  With Thee have I hidden myself.
Teach me to do Thy will,
  For Thou art my God;
  Let Thy good spirit
  Lead me in an even land.
For Thy name's sake, O Lord, *quicken me;*
  In Thy righteousness bring my soul out of trouble.
And in Thy mercy cut off mine enemies,
  And destroy all them that harass my soul;
  For I am Thy servant. (Psalm 143)

Although David served as a prominent king in Israel's history, his psalms frequently demonstrate that he was conscious of his humble status before God. In Psalm 143:1–2, David pleads for mercy, asks God not to judge him, and states that no human is righteous before God.

And yet, in these verses, David also asks God to listen to him: "Give ear to my supplications; in Thy faithfulness answer me" (verse 1).

The first two verses of the psalm exemplify a common Jewish understanding of the God who is both father and king. As a father, God hears us with love and forgiveness. As a king, God judges our actions and corrects us.

David first asks God to protect him from a relentless foe, probably King Saul (1 Samuel 18), who continuously pursues David. David says his spirit is crushed and that he feels like he's been forgotten in the darkness of the grave, "as those that have been long dead" (verse 3). The darkness David refers to may also be related to his time of hiding in a cave (1 Samuel 22). David is inwardly tired, and his heart is "appalled" (verse 4).

But then David turns his view away from his inner struggles and toward the work of God's hands. He doesn't refer to a specific action of God, but he says, "I remember the days of old; I meditate on all Thy doing; I muse on the work of Thy hands" (verse 5). We might say that David is moving out of introspection—a focus on his own difficulties—and toward a focus on God and all his works. In verse 6 David recognizes his need for God and says,

"I spread forth my hands unto Thee; my soul [thirsteth] after Thee, as a weary land."

Rather than trusting in himself, or perpetually studying his own soul, David trusts God to save him from his enemies (verse 9). David seeks refuge and consolation for his soul by persisting in deeply personal interactions with God (verse 8). So vital is this relationship with God to him that David believes he will descend "into the pit" if God turns his face away (*hester panim*) from him (verse 7).

In addition to a request for protection, David also asks God to teach him and lead him on level ground, "in an even land" (verse 10). In this verse, we might conclude that David is not relying on his own interpretations but seeking God's solutions to the difficulties in life.

As this prayer closes, David entreats God to free his soul from trouble and distress—for the sake of God's name (verse 11). In this statement, David's focus is on God's purposes. The last words of the prayer emphasize David's humble posture before God: "For I am Thy servant" (verse 12).

PRAYER

Blessed be the name of the Sovereign of the universe. Blessed be your crown and your abiding place. Let your favor rest with your people Israel forever: show them the redemption of your right hand in your holy temple. Grant to us the benign gift of your light, and in mercy accept our supplications. May it be your will to prolong our life in well-being. Let me also be numbered among the righteous, so that you will be merciful unto me, and have me in your keeping, with all that belongs to me and to your people Israel. You are the one who feeds and sustains all; you are the one who rules over all; you are the one who rules over kings, for dominion is yours.

I am the servant of the Holy One. Blessed are you, before whom and before whose glorious Law I prostrate myself at all times. I don't put my trust in people, nor upon any angel do I rely, but upon the God of heaven, who is the God of truth, and whose Law is truth, and whose prophets are prophets of truth, and who abounds in deeds of goodness and truth. In him I put my trust, and unto his holy and glorious name I utter praises. May it be your will to open my heart unto your Law, and to fulfill the wishes of my heart and of the hearts of all your people Israel for good, for life, and for peace.

Constant Gratitude

[A Psalm of] praise; of David.

I will extol Thee, my God, O King;
And I will bless Thy name for ever and ever.

ב

Every day will I bless Thee;
And I will praise Thy name for ever and ever.

ג

Great is the LORD, and highly to be praised;
And His greatness is unsearchable.

ד

One generation shall laud Thy works to another,
And shall declare Thy mighty acts.

ה

The glorious splendour of Thy majesty,
  And Thy wondrous works, will I rehearse.

ו

And men shall speak of the might of Thy tremendous acts;
  And I will tell of Thy greatness.

ז

They shall utter the fame of Thy great goodness,
  And shall sing of Thy righteousness.

ח

The LORD is gracious, and full of compassion;
  Slow to anger, and of great mercy.

ט

The LORD is good to all;
  And His tender mercies are over all His works.

י

All Thy works shall praise Thee, O LORD;
  And Thy saints shall bless Thee.

כ

They shall speak of the glory of Thy kingdom,
  And talk of Thy might;

ל

To make known to the sons of men His mighty acts,
And the glory of the majesty of His kingdom.

מ

Thy kingdom is a kingdom for all ages,
And Thy dominion endureth throughout all generations.

ס

The LORD upholdeth all that fall,
And raiseth up all those that are bowed down.

ע

The eyes of all wait for Thee,
And Thou givest them their food in due season.

פ

Thou openest Thy hand,
And satisfiest every living thing with favour.

צ

The LORD is righteous in all His ways,
And gracious in all His works.

ק

The LORD is nigh unto all them that call upon Him,
To all that call upon Him in truth.

He will fulfil the desire of them that fear Him;
He also will hear their cry, and will save them.

The LORD preserveth all them that love Him;
But all the wicked will He destroy.

My mouth shall speak the praise of the LORD;
And let all flesh bless His holy name for ever and ever.
(Psalm 145)

P salm 145 is the most revered psalm in the Jewish tradition. It is used every day to open the *Mincha*, or afternoon service. The name of the prayer, *Ashrei*, is based on the first word of Psalm 84:5, meaning "happy."

As we have seen, many of David's psalms poetically reveal his confessions, pain, laments, confusion, and fears. But in this psalm, David's focus is on God and the rewards of placing one's faith in him. It can be seen as an expression of joy, a psalm of gratefulness to God.

In verses 1 and 2, David vows to praise God forever. Perhaps David is sharing his desire to praise God in eternity. He could also be referring to his dynasty, which

God promised him, along with being the ancestor of the Messiah (2 Samuel 7:11–16). In verse 2, David promises to praise God every day, something his people have done using this prayer for thousands of years.

David carries his theme of God's lasting purposes into the next verses, saying, "One generation shall laud Thy works to another, and shall declare Thy mighty acts" (verse 4). David is probably referring to the Torah's admonition to teach each generation about God, which is found in Deuteronomy 11:18–19: "Fix these words of mine in your hearts and minds; tie them as symbols on your hands and bind them on your foreheads. Teach them to your children, talking about them when you sit at home and when you walk along the road, when you lie down and when you get up" (NIV). David speaks to his son Solomon about God and the Torah several times in the Bible: "And you, my son Solomon, acknowledge the God of your father, and serve him with wholehearted devotion and with a willing mind" (1 Chronicles 28:9, NIV).

In his prayer in Psalm 145, David says that God is "good to all; and His tender mercies are over all His works" (verse 9). These words can sometimes be difficult to understand, especially for those who have gone through significant hardship and suffering. We find the same questions being raised in relation to Psalm 145:15–20, in which David says God provides food to the hungry (verse 15) and "will fulfill the desire of them that fear Him" (verse 19).

As we have seen, David has experienced severe suffering (deaths of his sons, threats to kill him, and so on), and yet he still writes that God is good to all. This doesn't appear to be a simplistic statement, for when David suffered injustice under Saul and the betrayal of his son Absalom, he doubted God's presence in his life (Psalm 13:1–2, for example).

As with David, many people go through times when God's compassion and goodness are *not* apparent. So how, in this psalm, is David rectifying this apparent contradiction?

There are several responses from Jewish theologians. One possibility is that David is prophesying about the world of the future, a world in which all these verses become a complete reality. This is the world that we strive to build now in partnership with God and each other, but it has not yet been fulfilled by God. In other words, David is expressing his longing and hope for what is to come.

Another theory is that David is only writing in this psalm about the provisions and goodness of God, not about the hardships and suffering in the world. In this view, David chooses to focus on God's goodness, even though harsh realities of life may surround him.

Joy and celebration can be seen throughout Psalm 145. While considering this prayer, perhaps it is worthwhile to ask how we can be thankful and joyful even as we seek to overcome adversity and hardship.

After the reading or study of the Psalms, it is traditional to say the following prayer: "Come! Let us sing joyfully to *Adonai,* let us call out to the Rock of our Salvation. Let us greet Him with thanksgiving, with praiseful songs let us call out to Him. For a great God is *Adonai,* and a great King above all heavenly powers" (Psalm 95:1–3).

PRAYER

After reading Psalms, the following blessing may be said:

Baruch Atah Adonai, blessed are you, O Lord our God, King of the universe, Rock of all worlds, righteous through all generations, O faithful God, who says and does, who speaks and fulfills. All your words are truth and righteousness. You are faithful, O Lord our God, and your words are faithful. Not one of your words will return void, for you are a faithful and merciful God and King. We praise you, O Lord God; you are faithful in all your words.

Have mercy upon Zion, for it is the home of our life, and save her that is grieved in spirit speedily, even in our days. Blessed are you, O Lord, who makes Zion joyful through her children.

Gladden us, O Lord our God, with Elijah the prophet, your servant, and with the kingdom of the house of David. Don't allow a stranger to sit upon his throne, nor let others any longer inherit his glory; for you swore unto him that his right should not be quenched forever. Blessed are you, O Lord, the Shield of David.

---

museum of the Bible

Experience the Book that Shapes History

Museum of the Bible is a 430,000-square-foot building located in the heart of Washington, D.C.—just steps from the National Mall and the U.S. Capitol. Displaying artifacts from several collections, the Museum explores the Bible's history, narrative and impact through high-tech exhibits, immersive settings, and interactive experiences. Upon entering, you will pass through two massive, bronze gates resembling printing plates from Genesis 1. Beyond the gates, an incredible replica of an ancient artifact containing Psalm 19 hangs behind etched glass panels. Come be inspired by the imagination and innovation used to display thousands of years of biblical history.

Museum of the Bible aims to be the most technologically advanced museum in the world, starting with its unique Digital Guide that allows guests to personalize their museum experience with navigation, customized tours, supplemental visual and audio content, and more.

For more information and to plan your visit, go to museumoftheBible.org.